WOMEN IN VIETNAM

WOMEN IN VIETNAM

WOMEN IN VIETNAM

RON STEINMAN

TV Books

NEW YORK

Library of Congress Cataloging-in-Publication Data
available upon request from the publisher

Interviews courtesy of ABC News Productions

TV Books, L.L.C.
1916 Broadway, Ninth Floor
New York, NY 10019
www.tvbooks.com

Interior design by Rachel Reiss
Manufactured in the United States of America

DEDICATION

For all the women in these pages.
For all the women who served in Vietnam.
For all the women still to emerge from the shadows.

CONTENTS

One guy asked me, "Am I going to die?" I said, "Do you feel like you are?" He said, "Yeah, I do." I said, "Do you pray?" He said, "Now I lay me down to sleep." I said, "Good, that will work." He said, "Would you hold my hand?" I said, "I'll do better than that," and I got into bed with him. I put my arms around him and I brushed his face and brushed his hair and I kissed him on the cheek, and we said, "Now I lay me down to sleep," and he died in my arms calling me Mama. I wrote to his mother saying he did not die alone, and he called me Mama. I never heard back from her, but hopefully that thought has comforted her over the years.

Diana Dwan Poole
Army Nurse
Qui Nhon, South Vietnam, 1969–70

AUTHOR'S NOTE

During the war in Vietnam, American women were seemingly everywhere and nowhere at the same time. I was an American journalist and bureau chief with NBC News for twenty-seven months in 1966, 1967, and 1968. I was also there during parts of 1969, 1970, and 1971. As with all the other journalists, I was aware that "in country" or "on the ground" or however we may word it, were nurses, WACs, Red Cross volunteers, entertainers, missionaries, and civilians attached to American government agencies. There were never that many and the women were not all in the same place at the same time. They were all over the country, sometimes in groups of two and three, where they were needed and where they felt they had to be to support the troops and the war effort. But although women were in Vietnam, it did not mean that my bureau, or any other bureau, covered them with regularity. We did the obligatory story now and then, covering mainly the nurses and sometimes Red Cross volunteers, but rarely any other women. And we covered the war itself and the men fighting it. At the time, everything else seemed more important. Today, almost thirty years after the war, and as important as the men were, the women loom large because the American people have been remiss in their appreciation of what the women did during the war.

In 1999, I suggested a documentary on women in Vietnam as part of a new "Soldiers' Story" series produced by ABC News Productions for TLC. I wanted an hour on the air celebrating women that would help relieve my guilt for not providing the American public with more stories about these unsung heroes, who will tell you they were just doing their job. ABC and TLC agreed and TLC aired the compelling hour on February 7, 2000, to an appreciative and sizeable audience. This book is a result of that hour, but the book is different. Television, by its nature and time constraints, speaks in shorthand. How else can you fit eleven women into forty-five minutes and tell the story of women at war? So I took the eleven interviews, along with four women interviewed for, but not shown in, the documentary, and edited them for content and clarity while retaining the rhythm of their speech. I interviewed each woman more than once for her personal history before the war and to discover what she has been doing since. Thus the book contains a fuller treatment of the women and how the war affected their lives than what was seen in the documentary.

First, though, I have some deeply vivid memories to share. Then I will describe the women, who they were and where they served, as a prelude to their harrowing, powerful, moving stories.

INTRODUCTION

First you hear the sound of rotor blades somewhere off in the distance. It is distinct and steady, thwap-thwap, a sound like no other. Out of sight but coming closer, the sound magnifies anxiety. Hospital field phones have been ringing off the hook. There has been action, a firefight, and, again, too many wounded young men. Doctors, nurses, medics, and the hospital staff know the injured, maimed, and mutilated are coming. The choppers appear in the sky as if by magic. One, two, three, four Hueys arrive, sweeping in, as many as it takes—the number different each time, depending on the magnitude of the battle. The helicopters hover and land. Men and women—yes, women—the medical staff, run out under the still spinning rotor blades, the backwash whipping up the wind, to help unload the wounded.

In Vietnam I watched helicopters filled with wounded, dying, and dead land on helipads in safe landing zones far from the bloody battleground where the young soldiers fell. At the 3rd Field Hospital, Tan Son Nhut, I saw the sky darken with wave after wave of arriving Dustoff helicopters carrying wounded from another newly christened battlefield. I saw the same in Pleiku and Danang, unforgettable sights in a war filled with more than its share of harsh memories. After a fire-

13

fight, Dustoff helicopters were always last to land on or near
the battlefield. Normally the action was too intense, the incoming fire too hot, for the chopper to land safely in the midst
of the killing zone. Before helicopters could touch down, they
had to wait for troops on the ground to cut a landing zone (LZ)
in the jungle or to fashion one on a mountainside. In the
Mekong Delta, choppers had to land where they could, usually in rice paddies or on top of narrow earthen dikes. The ap-
proach was always difficult. When the landing zone was
ready, the helicopters swept in to drop needed supplies. Once
the "birds" were empty, the walking wounded made their way
to the narrow, lightly-armored, thin-skinned helicopters. Litters with the more seriously wounded waited as far away as
possible from the still-whirling rotary wings. Any GIs on the
ground who were still able became the litter bearers, waiting
for the best moment to fill the choppers. Then they'd rush
across dangerous terrain, working very fast to shove as many
wounded onto the helicopter as it could hold. Full, the helicopters lifted off, carrying out the wounded, usually under incoming enemy fire. Often within twenty minutes of liftoff the
helicopters arrived at a hospital, carrying wounded to their
first step of recovery.

In Vietnam, fewer men died of their battlefield wounds than
in any previous war because of Dustoff helicopters and well-
equipped modern field hospitals. The percentage who died of
their wounds declined from 29.3 percent in World War II to
26.3 percent in the Korean War to 19 percent in Vietnam.
Dazed and battered, the walking wounded emerged first from
the helicopters. Wrapped in hastily improvised battlefield
dressings, their uniforms torn and dirty, these bloody young
men resembled refugees from the Apocalypse. Often confused, their morphine wearing off or already out of their sys-

tem, they stumbled from the helicopters and made their way inside to the waiting nurses and hospital staff. They had entered the heart of triage, where, to the nurses in charge, they were obvious candidates for life. The walking wounded were easier to deal with because they were still partly whole. Though shot or wounded by enemy bullets or shrapnel, they could walk. Once off the chopper, they did so with purpose, unhurried, knowing the war was over for them, at least temporarily. Those on stretchers were another matter. They had IVs hanging from improvised poles attached to their litters. Bound in strips of gauze and tape, they were the badly wounded. With their torn and shattered bodies they often had little hope of surviving. These were young men with death hovering over them, waiting to strike.

Casualty clearing hospitals, those closest to the action, were small. Some field hospitals were not much bigger. And as small as any hospital may have been, it always looked larger than it was. Wards in larger hospitals seemed more spacious than they were. The uniform rows of beds filled with recovering GIs gave the wards a strange feeling of endlessness. The window panes were covered with strips of white tape in crisscross patterns to prevent flying glass if an enemy shell smashed into the hospital. It was common, not exceptional, for hospitals to come under enemy fire. But although physical danger was always present, you would never know it from the calm demeanor of the nurses. Away from home, often for the first time, frightened, with no relief from the horrors of war, nurses went about their business as if they were in the heart of Des Moines instead of in the middle of a war zone.

I found it difficult to look down a ward and see all those beds filled with bandaged soldiers. It was a shock to behold all that wasted youth. Those impressions echo in me to this day.

In Vietnam I visited hospitals more frequently than I wanted to, sometimes to see one of my staff recovering from a war wound, or malaria, or even a heart attack. Other times I had to be in a hospital for a briefing by a general, to watch a member of Congress or a government official on tour, or to cover a story, usually of heroism. Often I found all I could do was hold my breath. Looking at those battered young men I feared being poisoned by the wounds of war. Here were young men, American youths far from home, fighting in a war few if any of them understood. After surviving the cauldron of fire, they were in clean, white sheets wearing clean, white bandages. Here, with the help of nurses and doctors, they gathered their strength as they worked as hard as they could to survive their injuries. They were recovering from wounds, psychological as well as physical, that in some ways would never heal. Under heavy sedation they waited for the next repair job. Would it be another operation or the removal of stitches or that million-dollar flight, the one that would take them on their journey home and hoped-for recovery? Inside a hospital, especially after landing in the safety of an American base, no matter how serious the injuries, they had hope. Nurses carried that ray of hope for them. As you will see in these pages, these women were honest and just, hard-working and dedicated, sometimes angry, and filled with emotions they could not allow anyone, especially their patients, to see. They never willingly gave in. Rarely in starched whites, most often in fatigues, they padded silently from bed to bed, ministering to the wounded and praying silently.

Though people are familiar with the number of men who served in the military during the Vietnam War, few of us know anything about the women who served in South Vietnam. That is because they were all but invisible to the public, except to the people with whom they interacted every day. Ralph Ellison said his invisible man was invisible "simply because people refuse to see me." Many Americans did not want to see, or recognize the women, military and nonmilitary, who dropped out of the sky into that strange land. Because of the war, many women remain silent. They still fear facing the reality of their experience. In Vietnam, scores of women survived by denying the reality of the life around them. In Vietnam, they created a reality of their own so they could survive the rigors of war. The life they led in South Vietnam as women at war had been so foreign that, when they came home, relatives and friends would not acknowledge they had been there. But nothing will ever change what they went through. No matter what they felt, they served with honor, without complaint, and with distinction.

We know that the young men who touched down on South Vietnamese soil had their lives changed forever in ways they are still discovering. More than half the returning troops suffer from some form of post–traumatic stress disorder (PTSD). We know very little, though, about the women who went to war. They, too, changed in ways they are still discovering. Estimates are that as many as 25 percent have "service-connected" disabilities. Their memories, though vivid and searing, never completely describe the reality of each woman's experience. For those who knew battle, "the wheel of war never stops." Buddhist in sentiment, it is especially appropriate to the Vietnam War. In many ways the phrase applies to all the women who served in Vietnam. The wheel of memory still spins for them, twenty-five years after the last American departed the country. For the war they served in, the lives they tried to preserve, and the lives they tried to give hope to, that wheel keeps turning, and probably always will. It is a wheel of memory that includes all the wars of the twentieth century. It is eternal and infinite.

With 2.6 million men fighting a war, it is easy to understand how some Americans could be oblivious to the presence of American women in Vietnam. The women were there, though—on the front lines, on the bases, and in the cities, towns, and villages. They wanted to be in the war because they felt a need to help. They were believers in their country and in America's justification for being in Vietnam. They journeyed thousands of miles to that beleaguered land to serve their country, and to help the men who needed their support. They had heard from friends and enemies and the media that going to Vietnam was a political gesture in support of the United States. However, it made no difference to them. While there, they helped the best way they knew by giving everything they had, seven days a week, twenty-four hours a day. In time, many women came to understand that perhaps the cause they supported was weak, but while in South Vietnam, their role was not political. They returned home, silently and without fanfare. For many women, though, facing the realities of the war would not take place until years later.

Throughout World War I and World War II, the Korean War and Vietnam, the best estimates are that there were more than one million women in the military. For Vietnam, the numbers are small, though the war was the longest in American history, and they are not very accurate. In the period from 1962 to 1973, the years during which American troops were in Vietnam, 265,000 women served in the armed forces all over the world. For reasons that are still unclear, there are no records in the Department of Defense specific to women. Sources in the DOD tell me that "official records did not in any way define women as women." Military records give only a person's name. There is evidence that even when the person's name was a woman's, her official designation was "M" for male, not "F" for female.

The Pentagon was either gender-blind during Vietnam or the omission was deliberate. We will never know. Either way, as I have said, the military did not define women as women, something women veterans have been battling for the last thirty years. The Department of Defense, sources tell me, "had no central file that in bureaucratic terms discriminated between men and women." On a cold January day in 2000, I made telephone calls to United States government archives across the country. I spoke to two women who were in the public affairs office at the Pentagon, one who handled current affairs, the other who dealt with the Vietnam era. Neither had any information of value. In College Park, Maryland, I spoke with two people in the National Archives and Record Administration and they could not help. They had unit records and after-action reports, but no individual records. In St. Louis I talked to an archivist at the Center for Records. She only had individual records, not unit records, and unless I had specific details (name, unit, rank, year served, serial number) she could not begin to assist me. I also talked to two people in different sections of the Defense Manpower office. One had nothing and the other could only give me the data on the 58,209 dead from the war.

The Veterans' Administration could give me some numbers. The VA said that approximately seventy-five hundred women served in South Vietnam. "Approximately" because even their records are incomplete and probably always will be. According to the National Vietnam Veterans Readjustment Study conducted by the Department of Veterans' Affairs in 1988, the number of women "who were actually stationed or performed duty in Vietnam is not available." The study estimates that ten to eleven thousand served in Vietnam. The Veterans' Administration, however, has the following breakdown, which though too neat, can serve as a guide. Of the seventy-five hundred women, it can identify that 87 percent were nurses and they made up the vast majority. Approximately fifteen hundred were not nurses. Seven hundred women, enlisted and officers, were in the Women's Army Corps, known as WACs. There were fifty-four medical specialists, including dieticians and physical therapists. The navy had one hospital in South Vietnam and two hospital ships anchored offshore, but nine navy women were not nurses. Only thirty-six enlisted and officers were in the marine corps. At least five hundred women served in the air force. Because the air force housed them, or "outstationed" them, in Thailand, the Philippines, and other places in Southeast Asia, it is impossible to know how many served in Vietnam "on the ground." The air force is not specific about where the women served. Many were flight nurses and some of these nurses worked at "in-country" staging facilities and were rarely in Vietnam for more than a week. Of all the military women serving in Vietnam, 85 percent had enlisted and 90 percent were officers. According to the VA study, of the women who served in Vietnam, the best estimates are that 5.8 percent suffered wounds in all situations, 1.3 percent were wounded in combat, and 1.2 percent received the Purple Heart. Ironically, WACs as we knew them no longer exist. In October 1978, Congress disbanded the Women's Army Corps and integrated women into their respective branches, such as Intelligence, Ordnance, and Military Police.

Nurses ranged in age from twenty-two to twenty-five years, the average being only twenty-three. They comprised the youngest group of medical personnel to have ever served in a war zone. One third had just graduated from nursing school and were new to the military. For many, it was their first real job after graduation. Eighty percent of all the nurses in Vietnam were in the Army Nurse Corps. As young as the women were, the men they cared for were even younger, their average age only nineteen. Though rarely present for the violence, mutilation, and terror of war, nurses saw more death and destruction than any other group. They treated more than 350,000 wounded as nurses always do, direct, hands-on, with all the care and skill they could muster. Their only complaint was they never had enough supplies or enough help to do their jobs properly. They were the unfortunate heirs of the consequences of battle. Their responsibilities far exceeded their training as nurses at home, what they called "stateside" and the troops called "back in the world." From the day they landed in Vietnam at Saigon's Tan Son Nhut Airport, their lives were permanently altered. Assigned to the most stressful work possible, intensive care, operating rooms, triage, crippling wounds, severe burns, and amputations became commonplace and impossible to avoid. In field hospitals scattered across the country they became caregivers to the survivors of war's carnage. They found themselves living in outlying areas with strange names such as Danang, An Khe, Chu Lai, Dong Tam, Nha Trang, Qui Nhon, and Phu Bai. Among others, they worked at the 1st Medical Battalion, the 43rd Medical Group, the 85th Evacuation Hospital, the 8th Field Hospital and in medical units everywhere. The nurses in these units often provided the intermediate step to more intensive care before the wounded flew out on medical evacuation transports for further treatment in Japan, Okinawa, the Philippines, and America. In these pages you will read what it was like to have the wounded arrive at their field hospitals and evacuation hospitals, often in large numbers, after midnight and many times at dawn. Now, more than thirty years later, these nurses recall everything as if it were yesterday. They tell of their pain working triage, when they had to decide if someone might die because the body in front of them had been destroyed beyond any hope of survival. They had to choose who might live, and what treatment the living would get. One nurse says, "We put the bodies back together as best we could." It was, and still is, a frequently heard mantra.

Trained to do their jobs well, they had to be very tough to survive. Still, they had, as do all nurses, to show warmth and humanity, often when they knew they could do nothing to help the wounded. Nurses were stand-ins for girlfriends, wives, mothers, and sisters but rarely knew the names of the wounded they treated. They knew that a soldier died before the mother or father knew, before the family back home knew, and that was a difficult burden to carry. They knew faces and not much else; nurses recognized a man by the color of his hair and eyes, the shape of his nose, the cut of his jaw. Mostly they identified the man by his wound. But no matter what they did to help, the men kept dying. One nurse, Diana Dwan Poole, describes all the men she cared for as her "little brothers," an apt term that describes the emotional investment she had in her patients even when she knew, feared, they had no chance of surviving. Being almost the same age as the men they treated, it was easy for the nurses to identify with their wounded. Imagine, if they were not nursing them, they might have dated them, danced with them, bowled with them, gone to the drive-in with them, attended homecoming with them.

We should not forget that there were other women in Vietnam whose numbers are even more difficult to tally than women who were in the military. Again, these are estimates, mostly anecdotal, with hard figures impossible to verify. Depending how they calculate it, independent researchers use a low figure of four to five thousand women and a high of fifteen thousand. Some people believe as many as twenty thousand nonmilitary women may have been in South Vietnam, but not all at once. There were women missionaries frequently in and out of the country, usually for short periods, so their multiple visits give us the higher, but inaccurate, count.

Women were in the foreign service in administrative positions at the American Embassy, with USAID, and with the CIA. They were with Military Assistance Command Vietnam (MACV) and were part of the United States military civilian work force, known as DACS, the Department of Army Civilians. Women volunteered for the Red Cross, and were with Armed Forces Radio and Television. Women worked for the Peace Corps, the International Volunteer Service, and many small charitable groups. WACs helped train and advise South Vietnam's Women's Army Corps.

USO, officially the United Services Organization, ran recreation centers across Vietnam. USO workers and entertainers often lived in housing outside the military bases. They never wore uniforms, but dressed in civilian clothing. They traveled by jeep, truck, and helicopter from base to base. These volunteers went to USO centers like the Aloha Coffee Bar in Cam Ranh Bay, to China Beach, and the seaside resort town of Vung Tau, south of Saigon. They were in the same danger as everyone else in Vietnam.

We have seen pictures of them in Universal newsreels, in "The March of Time," in World War II documentaries, and Hollywood movies. We saw them standing behind tables in tents and mess halls, and on bases and in fields across Great

Britain and Europe. There, they handed out freshly baked donuts and coffee, dispensed good cheer, and raised morale. They are the Donut Dollies, whose name originated in World War II when they baked and served their donuts to legions of American soldiers in war zones across the world. In Vietnam, these women, only twelve to thirteen hundred in all for the war years, brought card games and board games and Kool-aid out into the field so the GIs had a touch of home. Officially called SRAO—Supplemental Recreational Activities Overseas—they were only one of the three categories of Red Cross workers in Vietnam. Other Red Cross volunteers worked in military hospitals and helped soldiers when they faced an emergency such as an illness or the death of a loved one at home. As hostesses at camps spanning the country from Chu Lai to Tuy Hoa, from Pleiku to Xuan Loc, they often shared a soldier's happiness when he received joyful news from home, such as the birth of a child. Sometimes the Donut Dollies and other Red Cross volunteers wore an official uniform of sorts, while other times they dressed in military garb. They worked in recreation centers at major bases. As part of a mobile unit, they visited troops in the field at fire bases before and after combat. Everything they did made the troops feel a bit closer to home, to Mom and apple pie. One young woman says, "When I appeared at a base, sometimes the soldiers, many even younger than I, could only sit and stare without uttering a word. When a tired GI saw an American girl, me, wearing a skirt, it was more than he expected, especially in a combat zone." For that teenage soldier, far from home, hungry, dirty, and exhausted, seeing a Donut Dolly, often close to the action, changed his life, if only for a moment. She was as far from home as he was and it made a world of difference to him. His increasingly violent world of war seemed distant when that typical American girl just happened to drop by on a helicopter. Considering where he was, it was not a bad substitute for the drive-in.

All the women who served, whether nurses, Donut Dollies, WACs, USO volunteers, or foreign service staff, had a common problem when they came home. They often did not have the desire or the willingness to share their experiences with anyone outside their circle. Because so few of them had been in South Vietnam, there were even fewer friends or family at home to whom they could open their hearts. Even men who were veterans rarely, if ever, listened to them. So the women stopped talking and kept everything inside. It was only a few years ago that male veterans started to acknowledge women were in Vietnam at all. They knew nurses were there. They had to know that, but unless they had been wounded or were in need of medical assistance, for them these gallant women were always on the outside, as if they were figments of their imaginations. Most troops did not consider that a hospital was on the front lines, though the Viet Cong might have shelled it nightly. That attitude extended to the public. Many Americans seemed to care nothing about the women who served in the war. Many still do not. Worse, until recently most major studies on the effects of war on the psyche did not include women. It is time for a change.

Often overlooked are the women who died in Vietnam. Eight have their names on the Wall. Seven were army nurses, including one killed in action and one air force nurse. Thirty-seven female civilian employees died near Saigon in the crash of an air force evacuation transport carrying orphans from Operation Babylift on April 4, 1975. Sadly, it happened just days before Saigon fell to the onrushing North Vietnamese. Those women, mostly civilian employees of the American Embassy, volunteered to escort the Vietnamese children to new homes in the United States. The women in these pages believe their names should also be on the Wall. Other women died in Vietnam, including missionaries and volunteers with various charitable organizations. Including Operation Babylift, more than fifty civilian women lost their lives during the war. Women veterans also believe any woman who died since the end of the war belongs on the Wall. For the living, unfortunately, death continues to take its toll long after the war's end.

Troops returning from Vietnam came home in ones and twos, never together in large numbers the way they did in World War II. When they started coming home after 1968 and the Tet Offensive, when the war, as we know, was at its nadir in popularity, they felt like lepers. This helped lead to the returning soldiers' isolation. The women, too, came home alone and, often by their own choice, unrecognized. It is worth repeating that many women quickly realized that even friends and family refused to understand where they had been and what they had been doing, so they learned to shut Vietnam out of their lives. As they say in these pages, they did not want to face the reality of what they had been through. Women veterans often felt misunderstood and out of place in the world which they had been away from for a year and sometimes longer. The war exhausted them. They had worked long hours. They had witnessed horror and destruction. They had known fear. They had seen young men become old men fast. They knew the weariness and hopelessness of war. Many of these young women soon knew the pain and sadness of depression, but they kept it buried inside. Alone at home, there was nothing they could do to change their situations.

To survive, women often built strict defenses against their pasts. Those lasted only so long. Many women exhibited profound symptoms of PTSD and many still do. As did the men, they denied the memory of their lives in Vietnam. They managed to keep the pain and fear of those memories far below the surface. Unlike the men, however, who had a hard enough time making anyone believe they were suffering, no one at first believed that a woman could possibly have PTSD. And that is where everyone was wrong. The delay in understanding that women veterans (and in the term I include any woman who spent any time inside South Vietnam) could suffer prevented many of them from getting needed treatment. On coming home, they were anxious and angry. They had nightmares and they were lethargic. Suffering from survivors' guilt, much like the men I interviewed for my earlier book *The Soldiers' Story,* they, too, did not know how to cope when "back in the world." They had survived the war. They lived while others died. In the war, the women gave hope where often there was none, offering warmth and comfort in a world they had never expected to be part of. The society they supported and thought they had loyally embraced rejected them because they did the unusual. They went to war. Many women—nurses, WACs and those in nonmilitary roles—were under fire, shelled by enemy gunners, though they were never in direct combat. They manifest the same symptoms as men under fire, in combat and out on patrol. This does not mean all the women who served in Vietnam or who appear in this book have PTSD. It does mean there was neglect when there should have been sympathetic understanding. If that had happened, healing for many of the women would not have been unusual. Today, neglected women veterans could be on the way to healing, their pain and suffering finally alleviated. Instead, there are those still haunted by the scars of remembrance. Many women describe themselves even now, thirty years later, as uptight, high-strung, and anxious. When they came home from Vietnam, many women went into psychic hiding and that is where many are still, not even admitting they were ever in South Vietnam.

In 1991 I was a producer with NBC News on a magazine pro-gram called *Sunday Today*. A story crossed my desk about the Vietnam Women's Memorial Project and how the women fighting for it were getting close to choosing a design for a statue that would be built next to the Wall. The Vietnam Women's Memorial Project? I had no idea there was one, or that there would be a monument to honor the women who were in Vietnam. I looked into the story and learned of their struggle with the establishment and their fight for recognition. *Sunday Today* anchor Mary Alice Williams and I went in pur-suit of the story. Its centerpiece, and a driving force behind the memorial, was retired army nurse Captain Diane Carlson Evans. We visited Diane Evans at her home in Northfield, Minnesota, and we also filmed her in Washington, D.C.

More importantly, we talked to her about her drive to honor all women who served in Vietnam. "Until I visited the Wall for the dedication in 1982, I had no tears. All those years I had not cried over Vietnam. I cried when I reached Vietnam in 1968. After that, there were no more tears. I had to shut down to survive. Maybe I really wasn't really there. Maybe I made all this up. All the women I worked with . . . nobody knows we were there." Diane Evans quit nursing in 1974 after having un-settling flashbacks, though she did not know what they were at the time. And she began to wonder about her life in South Vietnam. She began to wonder about all those other women who were also there. She said, "It is important for the families to know. It is important for the children to know." Originally, she, like the women on these pages, told no one out of guilt for having survived and for fear of the criticism she would get for having served. After she visited the Wall, she and other concerned women veterans banded together and dedicated themselves finally to speak eloquently about their service during the Vietnam War.

After our story played, Diane Evans sent me a copy of *Visions of War, Dreams of Peace,* edited by Lynda Van Devanter and Joan A. Furey. In it she wrote words that I will always treasure.

May 30, 1991

Dear Ron,

With great respect for your work. You are a special friend to Vietnam women veterans. You will find in this book why your sensitivity and support is not only noble but critical.

Some need to read this book to know why the Memorial is important. You knew before the book.

Our thanks,
The Vietnam
Women's Memorial
Project, Inc.

My thanks,
Diane Evans
Army Nurse Corps
Vietnam '68–69

Though Diane Carlson Evans is not in this book, her spirit and dedication infuse every page. My hope is that no one will forget the importance, the role, and sacrifice of all the women who gave of themselves so freely to that endless war. In November 1993, in Washington, D.C., before a crowd of thousands, the media, the world, and the women veterans of the Vietnam War saw the dedication of the Vietnam Women's Memorial. It was surely the first step for many on their long road to recognition and recovery. And it is here in these pages that these women who served so honorably but received no recognition finally reveal the depth of their experiences.

THE NURSES

DIANA DWAN POOLE
ARMY NURSE

Diana Dwan Poole joined the army nurse program in her last year of nursing school. She says, "They gave us a couple of hundred dollars a month and we took an oath to serve." After graduating she had medical basic training at Fort Sam Houston in Texas. After three years in the army as a full-time nurse, in 1969 she finally accepted a tour of duty in Vietnam. She had come to believe it was where she belonged and where her training demanded she be. After arriving in Vietnam, 2nd Lieutenant Poole worked as a nurse at the 67th Evacuation Hospital at Qui Nhon, a port in II Corps on the South China Sea, Binh Dinh province. Qui Nhon was a major American military base, providing needed supplies, ammunition, and fuel to more than ninety-five thousand allied troops. She served two tours as a nurse.

All women volunteered. We weren't drafted.

I was in the army already. I joined when I was a senior in

nursing school. Then I went to Letterman Hospital at the Presidio, San Francisco. I was there for two years, because they kept sending me orders to go to Vietnam and I was told you didn't have to go. I turned them down, just tore them up, okay? So I stayed at Letterman General Army Hospital for two years, and I was taking care of Vietnam returnees, guys that had been sent back home, and I talked to a lot of nurses that had been there. I was thinking, "I'm missing something, a piece of history," so the third time I got orders I said, "Okay, I'll go." Thirty days later I was there.

I went in 1969 to 1970 and I didn't leave because my little brothers still needed me so I extended for another year. My little brothers, all of them. They were all my little brothers—all my patients were my little brothers.

I went to Travis Air Force Base to leave for Vietnam. What was weird is the plane was full of little brothers wearing fatigues. But we had to travel in Class A green uniform, high heels, nylons. Twenty-four hours on an airplane like that was really bad. The plane broke down in Guam, so it took me twenty-four hours to get there. I had no idea what I was getting into. None. I mean, I was going to be a nurse, that was it.

From the air, Vietnam was beautiful. I got off at Tan Son Nhut Air Base. When they opened that door, the stench and the heat hit me smack in the face and almost knocked me down. I couldn't believe it, it smelled so awful. It was really horrible, and hot. I got on a bus, went to Long Binh, and I was there for three days because they didn't know where they were going to send me. Finally, after the three days they sent me by helicopter to Qui Nhon, which is about 250 miles north. Then they tried to tell me that I was AWOL, absent without leave, because I didn't show up for three days. I said it wasn't my fault.

It was horrible. I was going, "I hate this, I really hate this," besides, I was dead tired. I had been up, awake for twenty-four hours, so I wasn't really with it. When I got there I went to bed. I had to have some sleep. I went to sleep in an old iron bunk. It was weird. I don't remember a whole bunch of it because I was so tired. I woke up and then I said, "Oh my God, what in the world have I gotten myself into?" It was so foreign. I mean, just starting off with the weather. The one thing, it was like I was invisible—nobody even recognized that I was there, and I was basically told nothing. I didn't know where to go, who to report to, nothing, and it was just real confusing, and I got scared.

Everyday was the same. Get up, go to work, come home, go to bed, get up, go to work, and we worked for a minimum of twelve hours a day.

At first I was the head nurse of orthopedics because I was a captain, rank gets you that kind of a business. Then I was head nurse in casualty receiving and triage, and that was bad. Just casualties right off the field, still in their uniforms, handing me their boots saying, "Ma'am, my foot is in there, could you sew it back on?" and it was, and we did, we sewed it back on.

There were too many of the wounded. We had one little guy on my ward that just came out of surgery. He had only one arm left. That's all he had left. He woke up from his anesthesia and said, "I want a wheelchair now." I went, "Wait a minute, he just had both legs and one arm amputated, right?" Well, actually Charlie amputated them for him, Charlie being the VC. He kept insisting, so we got him a wheelchair and he went wild in that wheelchair, doing wheelies and all kinds of stuff up and down the ward. One arm, that's all he had left, and I wonder to this day what he is doing, if he's still even alive. Do you realize how many people have killed themselves since then? The statistics have it to about twenty thousand now, and I'm wondering if he isn't one of them.

I remember them all, believe me. There was one that's my nightmare. We were under red alert because we were being mortared. The hospital was being mortared and they had mortared a couple of different bases around, so we had seventy-five in the casualty receiving. Being the head nurse, I had to run around doing triage, and that means I decided who's the worst, who's going to surgery first, who's last, who is not going to make it so put him in the corner because he's going to die. We always cut all their clothes off, because you didn't know where shrapnel was, it could go anywhere. So we cut all their clothes off and I couldn't find anything on this one kid, nothing, not a mark on him, and he had no wounds. He kept screaming and screaming, and I said, "Just be quiet, I have all these other guys," and he said, "Promise me I'm not going to die, you won't let me die." I said, "I promise you're not going to die." I never lied to them. If they were going to die, I told them, because, if you're going to die and all, you don't need somebody lying to you. And this kid wasn't going to die, he didn't have a mark on him, so I just said, "you're not going to die. Now shut up." A little while later I was taking care of another guy, and I looked over at him and his stomach is growing and I grabbed Rick, who was the doctor, and I said, "Rick, look at him." He went over, grabbed a scalpel, cut between his ribs, jammed his arm in there, and he pulled his arm out. It was all bloody, and he said, "He doesn't have a heart, he doesn't have anything, he's mush inside." And the kid pointed at me, and said, "You promised me that I wasn't going to die," and then he died. He had a little wound in the perineal area between his legs. He had been in a tank that ran over a mine and a little piece of shrapnel had gone up there, gone all the way through his body and turned everything into mush. I didn't find that little tiny wound, and there was nothing I could have done anyway, but he's my nightmare—"You promised me, you told me you wouldn't let me die." Well, that was only one.

I didn't survive. I am seeing a psychiatrist as we speak. It has torn up my life. It really has. Yeah, nightmares and the whole thing. That's what's coming out now. You push it down, because if you let go, you're in a straitjacket. So you just go, "Oh, well, stuff like this happens," and you keep on going. You keep it inside, because you have to and you can't let those guys down.

I thought because I took care of all these guys in San Francisco, it can't get any worse than this. Because I was mainly taking care of amputees, guys that had stepped on mines and that sort of thing, I thought, it can't get any worse. Boy, was I wrong. It was worse. When you're the head nurse of casualty receiving, when they're off-loaded from a helicopter, still have dirt all over them and their uniforms on, and their foot is in their boot or whatever, or they've got their leg lying across their chest to see if we can sew it back on, I mean, that was worse than San Francisco, and I didn't think it would get any worse than that.

As a nurse it was second nature. I once had a helicopter pilot captain. They had uniforms which were supposedly fireproof, and the helicopters were filled with JP4, which is a jet fuel—highly, highly flammable. If one crashed, it usually burned, and there were usually no survivors. Well this guy survived, and his helmet was melted into him. He obviously went to the corner, which is where I put the guys that were going to die. And I hated that corner. By that time there were five guys in the corner. There was no way to get that helmet off him without taking flesh down to the bone off. There was no way. It was totally melted. His helmet was melted into his skull, and all he wanted me to do was take a picture of his wife and kids out of his pocket so he could see it. He said, "I know I'm going to die, take care of the other guys." Oh, man, he had two beautiful little girls. That's hard. That was hard. That was the same time the kid was saying, "You promised you wouldn't let me die," and that was a bad day. I remember him real well, too, because I felt like I let him down but there was absolutely nothing I could do for him, nothing.

Then, on the other side of the room a general was screaming at me, "Get over here, captain," because he had something in his eye. And I went over there, and I shook my finger in his face, I said, "You shut the hell up." "I'm a general!" I said, "In the hospital you don't have any rank. I am the captain of the ship, I outrank you, shut the hell up. We've got little boys here dying and I don't care if you have something in your eye."

Doctors helped when we could find them. Usually they were in the operating room, so basically I had to do most of it myself. On a day when we got seventy-five wounded in all at once, yeah, we were understaffed, but not in general. See, the hospital was really neat because it was just total teamwork. If they found out the rest of the wards weren't real busy right then, they'd all flock in and help, or if they were off duty they'd get out of bed and come over and help. We all did that.

When I was on the orthopedic ward, I had to take care of POWs as well. With this POW on my ward the idiots that ran the place put him in the bed next to the kid that the POW had blown both legs off. Put them right next to each other. I had a fit. That kid is screaming, "Why is he there? He's the one that did this to me," and he's right in the bed next to him. And that POW kept spitting in my face.

I had to take care of him. We had to keep him alive for information, please. For interrogation and all that sort of thing, and I just couldn't believe that I had to take care of this guy and the kid next to him, whose legs he blew off. It was just unbelievable. And that guy kept spitting in my face and yanking out the IVs and I kept putting IVs back into him, he kept yanking them out. So I got on the bed and I tried to kill him, and that is very hard to admit. I had my hands around his throat and I was—I was trying to kill him. I mean, I just blew a gasket. My corpsman had to pull me off, so I went storming to the COs and I said, "I don't want another POW on my ward. There's an empty ward next door, put them all over there. I don't want them next to my boys any more. I just don't want them there. I'll take care of them, put them over on the next ward." They put them all over there but I never went over there and I made the corpsmen do it. I didn't care.

They're all my boys. See, I was twenty-three, and they were like nineteen, so they were my brother's age, my real brother's age. They were all my little brothers, as far as I was concerned. Every damn one of them looked like my own brother. I never remembered their names, I didn't want to. I didn't want to. But since then I've met fourteen of them. I went to D.C. this year, on Veterans Day, and Carl, my husband, and I were walking down the sidewalk, and I had my fatigue jacket on—by the way, this is the one that I wore in Vietnam—and we were walking down the sidewalk and here comes this guy running one hundred miles an hour down the sidewalk. Picked me up, grabbed me, threw me around, and he said, "You were my nurse on my nineteenth birthday, you brought me a cake." I said, "With a match in it." And he said, "Yes." I said, "That's you?" and he said, "Yes, I'll always be nineteen in my head, always, and I'll never forget you." I said, "How in the heck did you recognize me?" He said, "You look the same." The guy is like fifty years old now, but he said, "I'm always nineteen and I'll never forget you brought me a cake." I said, "It came out of a C-ration can." He goes, "I don't care, it was my birthday cake and you sang to me." So there are some good stories.

I saw a lot of them die, and none of them were easy, but believe me, they are in a better place than I am right now. Because they aren't going through all this stuff in the world. They're in heaven with God and having a good old time. As a matter of fact, I thought time would heal it, and I talked to a psychiatrist and he said, "It will never go away, it's part of you. If anything, it gets worse, unless you figure out how you can cope with it and live with it every day." He said, "It's like diabetes. It doesn't go away. It gets worse. You can control it and learn how to cope with it and live around it." But I haven't figured it out yet.

My mother keeps saying I need to be in a loony bin because I'm crazy, but what I have is called PTSD, which is post–traumatic stress disorder, and it's from something above and beyond normal living that you have survived. I did it for two years, every day, so that's like way above and beyond, and it's not crazy, it is not a mental illness, it is a stress disorder. A lot of people think I'm crazy, but call it crazy to you?

I have no idea how many I treated. I could say on a bad day there were seventy-five, on a good day I got none, but the hospital was full. We only kept them three days. We never had empty beds. I don't know how many . . . thousands, thousands. There are several that stick in my head, like the little guy that was bleeding to death. I will never forget that one. We did what was called DPCs, which is delay primary closure, which means when they went to surgery, they would not close the wound. Say they did an incision on the thigh, and they partially fixed it, and they would tie off the bleeders, that sort of thing, but they left it open, because we didn't have the facilities to do a decent job. I mean, there was dirt all over the place and bugs and all kinds of stuff. So they would wrap the wound in tons of gauze, all the way around the leg, and then within three days the guy was off to Japan or the Philippines and they'd finish the surgery there. This guy had both legs wrapped like that, he stepped on a mine or something, and the kid—he was the worst one there and I always put the worst ones right in front of my desk so I could keep an eye on them. I was working nights, which is from seven at night until seven in the morning. They only had two shifts, seven to seven or seven to seven. I was working the night shift, and this kid was right in front of me, and he kept going, "Captain, captain, something's wrong, something's wrong." I'd go over and there were no lights on, so I'd have to use a flashlight. He was paste white, and he said, "There's something wrong, I can feel stuff leaking." Like I said, he had these bandages that were so thick there wasn't anything on the outside of them, right? But it would take a lot of blood to soak through all of that. Finally it soaked through all of that and it was dripping on the floor, right, and this kid was paste white and he said, "I can feel it squirt every time my heart beats." That tells you that's an artery. In other words, he was pumping his life out, and I said, "Oh, my God." We didn't have a PA system, so I sent the corpsman running for the doctor, and he said, "I'm asleep, go away." So I typed his blood and crossed-matched it, ordered blood, had three units going, one in each arm, one in one leg, with blood pressure cuffs pumping it in. As fast as I pumped it in, it was running out on the floor. This kid was from Alabama, that's all I remember. My corpsman and I did that for probably five hours. The doctor would not come because the kid couldn't possibly have a bleeder because he did the surgery and it was perfect.

The doctor finally got out of bed, because it was seven in the morning by then, and he said, "Oh my God, how many units of blood did you put in him?" I said, "Thirteen," which is how much you have in your whole body, and he said, "Well, geez, I couldn't have missed a bleeder." I said, "You missed an artery." So he took him back into surgery and fixed it. It was an artery. It was the only time in my life a doctor has ever apologized to me, ever in my life. This guy, he looked at me, he said, "I am so sorry," and he said, "That kid would be dead if it wasn't for you." He said, "I promise you to this day, I will never doubt a good nurse's word again." He and I are still friends. He and I were together in San Francisco and we ended up in the same hospital in Vietnam and couldn't believe it. I still keep in touch with him. He lives out in Lake Tahoe.

That's what I was there for. I was doing my job just like they were. It wasn't a big deal. I don't think I have a halo or anything. I think about the ones that I lost most. And go, "What could I have done that maybe he'd be alive today?" That just kills me, thinking, "What else could have I done?" That's a killer. I dream about them at night and wake up in the middle of the night. All these years, yes, after all these years, and like I said, the doctor said it will never go away. So.

A guy said to me last year, "What are you doing wearing that shirt," this one, "You didn't earn it, so you don't get to wear it." I went, "Well, if you look at the label it says 'One Each OD, Women's Size Small,' and I don't think it would fit you. I earned it, all right." He said, "Well, there weren't any women over there." I said, "You're right, we were little girls, we weren't women. Were you ever wounded?" He said, "No," and I said, "Thank your lucky stars you never saw me, just thank your lucky stars, because if you had been wounded, you would have all of a sudden figured there were women over there, because you'd have seen us." He still told me I was lying. Then a woman came up to me and asked me, "How in the world did you keep your white uniforms clean over there?" "What white uniform? This is what I wore, same things the guys were wearing, jungle boots, you know, fatigues, no white uniforms."

I went to work a lot of times with my flak jacket and helmet on. We had red alert sirens going and I'd dive underneath my bed and slag out [get out] my flak jacket, put it on, and head to the hospital, because if there was red alert we were going to get patients. Under fire everybody comes streaming out and heads to the hospital. You could hear the mortars walking in. They walked in steadily and they kind of felt their way. They'd hit one here and go a few meters headed towards your place. Boom, boom, boom. Closer and closer. And I tell you what, now this is funny, but it's really true, because I was petrified. They were headed to the hospital and that's when I had seventy-five in there. By the way, to give you a picture of what casualty receiving was, it was a bunch of sawhorses set up on a concrete floor with concrete block walls. That was it. Stretchers were canvas things and they went on the sawhorses, and when they ran out of sawhorses we lined them up on the floor and you had to step over them. This incoming, you could hear it coming, boom, boom. I've got my flak jacket on, my helmet on, and I thought, "My God I'm going to hide under my desk and save myself." I went, "You can't do that, you're the nurse, you have all these guys. Well, I can't save them all, so I'll save the closest one," and I threw myself over the top of this guy. Know what he said? "Wow, I could get used to this," and I started cracking up. We were going to die any minute, right, and he's making jokes.

We knew the day we were going to leave when we got there. They gave you a date—this is the day you're leaving—or

DEROS is what they called it, date of estimated return from overseas. I was a captain and what they were getting over there was second lieutenants, which means fresh out of nursing school. They didn't know anything, had never worked as a nurse before, and they're going to work on my boys. Uh-uh, not unless I'm there to show you how to do it right, and besides, there were still more boys and they still needed me, and it was a worthwhile job. I told them I wanted to stay, and I already had orders to go to Germany. I was going to be the head nurse of an orthopedic ward in Germany. I had ordered a Porsche, it was waiting for me, and I was going to drive one hundred miles an hour down the autobahn. I was going to learn how to ski in the Alps. I turned all that down to stay for another year in Vietnam. But I didn't end up staying a year, I was only there six months because I got beaten almost to death by the guy that I married. He was a Dustoff pilot, an air ambulance, medevac helicopter, and he got shot down that day so he was in a bad mood, I don't know, he just started beating on me, and the next thing I know it was three days later. I had amnesia or blacked out or I don't know what. I was unconscious, and black and blue and everything, and I had a really bad head injury and they slapped me in my own hospital. I was there for a month, because I had a torn brain, basically, brain contusion, and they were afraid I was going to have a stroke, blood clot type of thing, and they sent me home. They sent me home because I couldn't stand up without blacking out.

I didn't want to leave and they tied me down because they didn't want my head to move. They put me, like so much cargo, in the back of a C-130, which is a cargo plane, next to all the other patients that were going to Japan. This kid next to me was dying, and I'm tied down, my hands are tied down. I was screaming at them, "Let me loose so I can take care of him or at least hold him as he dies." Nobody deserves to die alone. Nobody heard me, and the kid died right next to me. That made me so mad, because they had me tied down, I couldn't move. So I went to Japan and then I went home.

That was it, the end of my military career, because my husband told me I couldn't stay in any more. So as soon as I got to the hospital, same hospital that I left from in San Francisco, I was supposed to be admitted and he wouldn't let me be admitted. He told me, "You're getting out." I resigned my commission right there. They said, "But you have to be admitted to the hospital," and I said, "He won't let me." I didn't need to be beaten up again so that was it.

Do it again? Not real willingly, but because of the guys I would do it, not for my country, but for those boys who needed me. It was worth it. Because I know that there are guys walking around out there who have wives and families, that would not be walking around if they hadn't seen me or one of the other nurses. They would not be alive. I feel like I did something worthwhile.

People didn't want to hear about it when I came home. They don't even know anything about it. My mother won't even listen. You know what I got for Christmas in Vietnam? Dish towels and pot holders. What dishes? I had no dishes. I also got bubble bath. I didn't have a bathtub, exactly. They thought I was on vacation in the South China Sea or something, and they don't want to hear it today. Do not want to hear it! And they'll be the first to tell me, "I don't want to hear this."

We were there and we counted. There are guys, like I said, walking around out there that would not be walking around if it wasn't for the nurses in Vietnam. The USO workers and the Red Cross girls, they did their part too. They brought a little bit of home to these guys that were lonesome and homesick and in this strange, foreign country full of the enemy. We counted.

Born in Benton Harbor, Michigan, a town of about twelve thousand on Lake Michigan, Diana Dwan (below, with fellow veterans) was the daughter of a businessman and a housewife. She attended two different high schools and graduated from St. Joseph's Catholic High School in Stevensville, a few miles down the coast from Benton Harbor. She was

the Western Michigan Ball Queen and she became the Berrien County Apple Queen. Chosen Michigan Apple Queen, Diana toured the country to promote Michigan apples. After high school she attended the Bronson School of Nursing in Kalamazoo. When she returned from Vietnam, she worked as an RN, a registered nurse, but she quit three months later. She remembers her pay was $3.10 an hour but found herself in what she calls "an Alice in Wonderland World, where nothing was real." Nursing was far different at home than it was in Vietnam. She has held many jobs, only to leave each of them. Diana raised two children, divorced, and remarried, this time to a Marine veteran of Vietnam. She considers her only true friends her "little brothers," the men she cared for during her nursing years in Vietnam. Going to the increasingly popular, important, and life-affirming reunions held around the country for Vietnam veterans, Diana has met many men she nursed during the war. She currently lives in North Carolina.

LILY JEAN ADAMS
ARMY NURSE

While in her last year of nursing school, after being recruited by the army, Lily Jean Adams signed up for a tour of duty as an army nurse. She graduated at the age of twenty-one in 1968, and first served at Fort Ord, California. She then went to Vietnam and the 12th Evacuation Hospital in Cu Chi, an important United States Army base camp only thirty miles northwest of Saigon. There she worked in the intensive care unit and as a triage nurse. A major headquarters complex, Cu Chi had extensive storage facilities, living quarters, and hospitals with doctors and nurses. Cu Chi was also famous for its vast tunnel complex and many caves built by the Viet Cong. During the war U.S. forces barely penetrated this underground fortress. Today it is one of Vietnam's major tourist attractions.

When I was in high school, I was dating a guy who ended up getting his draft notice, and his friends and all the other boys were also getting draft notices. I listened to their conversation when they were joking around—"Should we go to Canada, ha ha ha, should we join the marine corps, the navy, instead of going in the army, should we wait and get drafted?" I watched how they couldn't get decent jobs because everybody felt that if they were trained they would be wasting their money because they'd end up going into the military. I started feeling guilty that I was a girl and I didn't have to worry about this serious decision that these guys had to make. About three years later, I ended up in nursing school and a nurse recruiter came in and talked to us about joining the military, and all these wonderful modern hospitals that we could be in. There must have been three of them, at the most, built in World War II. They were not modern. She said you could travel, and they showed this wonderful movie of how much fun it would be. They never did mention the Vietnam War, although it was going on at the time. This was 1967. I was graduating a year later from nursing school, in 1968, and I had no idea what I was going to do after graduation.

I always wanted to be a nurse. When I was very, very young, maybe five, I wanted to be a nurse. I wanted to help people, take care of people, and serve the universe. That was just something in my heart and I love it. I still miss nursing in a hospital, and I miss the old ways that we took care of patients. Now I'm a holistic nurse and trying to replicate all that I loved about nursing, which is taking care of people, educating them, and providing comfort.

A year before graduation they had offered to pay for the last year of nursing school if we joined then. I also was a John F. Kennedy person and I just felt it was one way of honoring him. So I kind of put it all together and justified joining up. When I did decide this, I asked the recruiter if I had to go to Vietnam, and she said, "Oh no, women volunteer to go to Vietnam." So, I thought, "Well, okay, that's a pretty good deal." I could take care of the guys when they come back stateside, because I really didn't want to go to war, and I didn't believe in the war. I felt something was fishy about it. I wasn't really well-educated in politics, but somehow it didn't feel right to me. My dad and I argued because I was under twenty-one when I signed up. He was in World War II, but I told him, "Well, the recruiter told me I didn't have to go to Vietnam unless I volunteered," so he signed. I found out later on, when I graduated from nursing school and entered basic training, that sure enough, they send nurses to Vietnam. My mom thought it was a good idea because I was in limbo. I had no idea what I wanted to do, where I wanted to go. It was just two years that I had to sign up for, and I'd get all this experience. So, what the hell. No one knew what the war was about. We saw clips on TV and I was too busy in nursing school studying to really pay much attention to the news. I was very naive, like most people my age. You didn't have to volunteer, and I did not volunteer. I did not want to go.

I was at Fort Ord for eight months, where I took care of a lot of guys that came back from Vietnam with bad, major fractures, complicated fractures, usually of their legs, and shrapnel wounds and things of that nature. I learned a little bit about war when I worked night shift or evening shift. Sometimes the guys would have really bad nightmares, they'd cry, they'd scream, and I'd sit with them and calm them down, and we'd talk a little bit. But they never really wanted to tell me too much about the war. They felt that it wasn't fair for me to learn the horrors of war. I was very curious to find out what this horror was all about, and they would say, "I just don't want to share this with you. It's not fair, you shouldn't know about this." It was kind of almost like an oath that they had made not to go beyond a certain boundary, and I understand it now. There's certain things I don't discuss. I don't want other people to know the horror, but I want people to know of the horrors of war so that when we do go to war people aren't so rah, rah about it, although they have been lately, real excited about us going to war and fight. But there are some things that are left for me to keep inside.

I have people close to me that want to know why I react a certain way. I'm willing to share some things, but I don't go into the gory details. It's kind of, "You don't really need my nightmares, you don't really need my intrusive thoughts." I know when I got my orders for Vietnam at Fort Ord, a lot of the guys had heard about it. It's a fairly small kind of hospital where word got around. I was one of the last of the nurses to get the orders. I just watched my friends get their orders and leave, and I was one of those left behind, and I thought, "Maybe they'll skip over me," but they didn't. They got me in just enough time to send me over for a year. I remember them approaching me and saying, "It's really not that bad, they need nurses desperately," and that was something they did know. I felt, "Well, if I'm really needed, I'm not going to fight this. I'll just go and see what it's about."

I got a new chief nurse around that time, and she kind of apologized. She said, "Everybody knows you didn't want to go." I made it very clear when I got to Fort Ord, "I don't need these orders, I don't want these orders, I'll do anything, but don't send me." She said, "They really need you there, there is a shortage of nurses, and I fought with them because there is a shortage of nurses at Fort Ord, too." I mean, there was a shortage of nurses everywhere. I found out many years later that because it was not a popular war a lot of women didn't join like they did in World War II or even during the Korean War. So when I heard I was needed, I felt that that was part of my deal of becoming a nurse: go where I'm needed. I had spent a number of years seriously thinking about being a nun, so serving humanity was part of what I believed my mission on the planet was, so I felt, "Well, yeah, I should go if I'm needed." And no, I don't regret going, I really don't. I know I was one of many people who helped save a lot of lives. But I was also affected by Agent Orange, and I've lost two children, and I have one child with a birth defect, and my daughter worries about having children with birth defects, because we know it affects other generations. We're up to the fourth generation and there are birth defects up to the fourth generation that we know of in great-grandchildren of Vietnam vets. So, in some ways, yes, I regret that I've created this genetic time bomb. I'm kind of stuck. I can't say I don't regret it, and I can't say I do regret it. I just look at both sides of the story.

My plane ride over was on American Airlines. I still, to this day, refuse to fly on it unless I absolutely have to and I avoid it the best I can. It may sound silly, but it's the principal. They gave us the same chicken dinners, we had five meals, the same chicken dinner, the same salad, same dessert, the same everything. The stewardesses didn't pay any attention to the women. If we asked the stewardesses for a pillow or a blanket, a glass of water, Coke, or anything, they didn't cater to us. So if we wanted anything we'd ask the guys to ask for it and they got it for us. It was that kind of thing.

In the military sexual harassment was very common. But I'd say—because we were nurses—we were kind of on a little bit of a pedestal, especially with your guys that were in Vietnam, or your staff that were in Vietnam. They had a great deal of respect for nurses, so I think we got the least of it as far as being women in the military compared to women who were maybe enlisted or in another field. I don't think that I dealt with as much harassment and discrimination as maybe in another area. In nursing, you're in so many years and you go up the ladder, up the ranks. You're given certain responsibilities because you're a nurse with so much experience. It's very different than if you were a clerk or a secretary or an X-ray tech or something like that.

October 31, 1969—Halloween—we went from Travis Air Force Base to Vietnam. As we're flying I was thinking, "Trick or treat, my government, thank you very much." It took me many years to get over Halloween night. Every time I heard "trick or treat" something would happen and I wasn't able to really identify that it was a trigger until many years later, of why I had an issue with Halloween and the term "trick or treat." Something like that sticks in your head when you're going through a process like this. We got into Hawaii at like eight in the morning, got off the plane for the plane to refuel and do what-not, and they told us to go into the terminal, which we did, where we had a decent breakfast. All of us were in the ladies room. Some of the women were primping and whatever, and I was standing there and I said, "We all could desert, we're still in the United States." About five of them turned around and said, "Shut up," and I thought, "Wow, I think I'm saying what these people are thinking and they didn't want it to be discussed because it would be a great temptation." The women I was traveling with did not want to go to Vietnam. Most of us were pretty angry, most of us had heard enough about the war from our patients for eight months and made our own decisions and had opinions about what was happening. We didn't like it, and it was too late. We were one of the last groups to go, and I remember everybody being very angry. Then we hopped to Guam and we went to Midway or Wake Island, and then finally Vietnam. I remember looking out the window and seeing all this green and thinking, "How could there be a war in such a beautiful country?" It was like this emerald in the middle of the ocean. We landed and it was hot and it was smelly and it was sticky. I remember I wanted to get off the plane, then feeling the heat and the smell at the doorway and wanting to turn around and go the other way. But everybody was coming *this* way, and getting into buses with those special screen windows. I thought, "The Vietnamese liked us. I think they wanted us to come here. Why do we have to be protected? Why do we have to be in a bus?" I remember turning around and these kids were bugging us, I guess they were begging, and I turned around and one of them did this with his finger [she gestures with her middle finger] as we drove away and I thought, "What is all this about? I thought they would be welcoming us. I thought they would be happy to see us, so what is this all about?" And I found out.

When we arrived at the terminal, there must have been, I don't know, a few hundred guys waiting to get on the plane to leave, and they were all harassing us. All the guys in one group were yelling at us, saying, "Short, we're short, ha ha, we're short, you're getting off *our* freedom bird."[1] I thought, "When I leave I'm not going to do that, I'm not going to do that to people coming off the plane, that's cruel," because they were really enjoying it, they were really getting off on it. I was feeling like shit to begin with, I didn't really need to feel worse by hearing them making fun of us. I can understand it now. I was watching them, and the most shocking thing was thinking that they were in their early twenties, and they looked like they were in their forties. Now, remember, in those days I thought forty was old. So, it's like now I'm in my fifties and looking at them and thinking that they look seventy. They had aged so much, and that scared me. I thought, "What did they see that they aged like this?" I

---

[1] "Short" means our time in this country is up.

knew that they weren't forty. I knew that they were nineteen, twenty, and that was kind of another warning to me about what was to come. When I finally left, I felt quite elated when I was there, on that same spot, waiting for my freedom bird. I couldn't wait to get out of that country and go home again.

We worked twelve-hour shifts, six days a week. When we first got there we were oriented to the triage, ICU, and recovery rooms. We did that just so we knew what it was all about, and we were told that these nurses had priorities and that they needed to sleep. If they had to work overtime, they would be calling us to help, help take care of patients in these areas and to replace the nurses that needed to sleep because these were such important areas to work in. My first day in triage we were pretty busy, and when they brought in the first casualties, there must have been five or six, I was stunned and shocked. I couldn't move. All I kept on doing was watching, watching these casualties come in. It was like watching a movie. I had never seen casualties like this before in civilian life. I'd worked in the emergency room, I'd seen automobile wrecks, but I hadn't seen casualties from war. They were dirty and bleeding. I mean bleeding. I was kind of shocked at my own reaction because I really couldn't focus, couldn't concentrate, and I just wanted to run out of there. Then they brought in a second group of people and again, I couldn't move, and I was told I was not really expected to function, I was just to observe, to see things. But by the time they brought in the third group of people, there weren't any nurses left. There weren't too many people left, and the doctor was screaming for somebody to help him hold this guy's head while he did CPR and I was thinking in my head, "I could do that, I can hold somebody's head." That's about all I could do at that point, but once I was able to hold his head, after that I was able to function. When they brought in the next group of people, I was able to move and do things. I had not started an IV at the time because in the hospital stateside nurses weren't allowed to start IVs, but here nurses were expected to start IVs. We were starting inter-caths, so we weren't starting just needles, we were starting big thick needles with a tube. You pull the needle out and the tube stays in, so it was a whole different kind of thing, only interns were allowed to do that. So I was doing things in triage that nurses stateside weren't allowed to do.

I did what I had to do. It took a while and I felt guilty about it, but everybody said, "Oh, everybody does this, don't feel guilty about it. Everybody's in shock in the beginning, and some people can do this and some people can't." I was assigned to intensive care after that where it was half burns and half the amputees with complications. The burns were severe burns, and that's where I met Jim Fleck. He had a head concussion from a rocket attack and there was no place to put him except in my ICU and so he was brought there. The other half were amputations with complications, usually double amputees with their legs blown off and chest wounds or belly wounds. Those were complications! If it were just amputees, then that wasn't a complication, but if it was any other kind of wounds, then they needed intensive care. So we had to take care of both sides. There are only two nurses during the day, and one medic. Our head nurse wasn't much help. She felt sitting at the desk was her job.

It was very hands-on. This was vital signs on a regular basis, and a lot of painkillers for the burns. We took care of children that were amputees with severe burns. We lost a lot of children from severe burns because we didn't have the technology that we have today. We lost a lot of people in those days that we could have saved had we known more. I took care of one Vietnamese woman who was 80 percent burned. She set herself on fire when she found out her GI boyfriend was going home without her. He had promised to take her with him. We got North Vietnamese POWs that we had to keep alive for the interrogators to talk to.

You get this person in a bed and he's the enemy and you're supposed to hate him, but how can you hate somebody when you don't really know what he's done? There was a really ugly doctor who was an orthopedic doctor. I remember him coming in, and he had this philosophy of scrubbing the end of the stump to prevent infection. We would give the patients a morphine IV so they'd be so stoned they didn't really care what the doctor was doing. The doctor came in and proceeded to do this scrubbing on this guy's stump. He was a North Vietnamese, and the Vietnamese are very quiet. They hide under the sheets because they're cold from the air conditioning in the hospital, so you forget them sometimes. You really do. There's a person in the bed but you're busy taking care of people who are squeaking. You know, the squeaky wheel—"Nurse, I need help." Of course our GIs speak English and they would call us, "Could you help me here, help me there?" So the Vietnamese, especially the POWs, kind of hid underneath the sheets hoping that nobody would notice them. They tried to disappear, so a lot of times I didn't ignore them on purpose but I'd forget about them because I'd be so busy. I remember this time when the doctor came in and I said, "What are you doing?" He said, "Well, I'm scrubbing his stump." I said, "Why didn't you warn me? I would have had the morphine ready." He goes, "Oh, he doesn't need morphine," and he proceeded to torture this man. I ran to Narcotics. Narcotics are locked up so you have to unlock the Narcotics door with your Narcotics keys and I was shaking trying to get everything together, trying to get the syringe. I was so angry at this doctor, I wanted to kill him. I ran over, put the IV in, and I was sick. I was so angry at the doctor. The doctor laughed the whole time. He thought it was so funny to watch me do this routine, and he left. I was quite shaken. Of course this poor man was quite shaken, too, but my GIs were also shaken. They gave me cigarettes and they said, "Give him a cigarette. Can you do anything more for him?" Instead of seeing him as the enemy, they now saw him as a fellow soldier with the same injury, and they had compassion. I thought, "Jesus, this is insane. Here I am in a war zone that probably got blown up due to this prisoner. Have enough compassion for him? What is war all about? Why do we have to be in war? I'm all confused. What does this all mean?" And I left shortly after that. I applied to go to triage because I felt I was getting too connected to my patients. I didn't want to see these stories before me. In triage, you're with them for five minutes and then they're gone. You don't know anything about them. When I went to triage, where I spent like eight months, I learned you don't need to spend a very long time with somebody to get to know them very well. Especially *your* men who are dying. That's a whole other story of spirituality. There's that spiritual aspect to dealing with people in triage that you don't deal with in other areas.

The North Vietnamese were highly respected because apparently what the men told me was they were excellent soldiers. The men didn't like the VC because they were sneaky. But of course they were peasants and they weren't well-trained and they just did what they did when they had the war with the French. So they fought primitively but they fought very well, even if it was in a sneaky way. I didn't have any issues with the Vietnamese. The Vietnamese were very kind, thankful people. When we took care of the children, their parents, usually a mama-san, came in and stayed with the children the whole time they were in the hospital. They helped feed them. Some-

times they would help pass trays out. They would help empty
garbage. They would help us, and in the beginning they would
sit for a day or two and observe us and then they would start
doing things. All of us are like, "Uh-oh, Mama-san's getting up.
What is she doing at three in the morning?" Then we'd realize
that she was starting to clean up or she would sweep, they
wanted to do something in return for what we were doing for
their children. They really did appreciate what we were doing.
The Vietnamese that were hired to pass out food and stuff like
that were very friendly and cheerful and in some ways they
kind of gave us another perspective of life because things were
pretty serious in a hospital situation, but they would come
with their cheerfulness.

I'm from New York City, and I had a very heavy New York
accent at the time. As soon as I opened my mouth, some East-
erner would go, "Oh my God, she's from New York City," and
I would be surrounded by New Yorkers. The men would say,
"Talk, just keep talking, it sounds so good to hear a New York
accent coming from a woman, just don't stop talking." We'd
talk about where I lived, what school I went to, did you know
so and so? It was that kind of rap session that would happen as
a result of my New York accent. But most of the time . . . some
people just assumed I was American because I was wearing a
uniform and running around the hospital. I was mistaken by
one NCO for being one of the interpreters, and he goes, "Aren't
you Sandy?" I said to him, "No, I'm not." He goes, "Oh, I'm
sorry." And because I said, "No I'm a nurse here," he was, "Oh,
I'm sorry, I didn't mean to do that to you." But the Vietnamese
assumed I was Vietnamese and they assumed I was an upper-
class Saigon woman that was an interpreter and thought she
was better than them. Cu Chi was an agriculture area, so they
were all peasants. I would have some older Vietnamese people

mad at me because I wouldn't talk to them, as much as I'd say, "No bic [pronounced like "speak"]," "no bic" means "I don't understand." The interpreter would say, "She's from America, she's American, she doesn't speak Vietnamese." The old ladies would go, "No, no, she's from Saigon. She just thinks she's better than us because she's from Saigon," so I got some of that kind of stuff. I was well-known in the compound and a lot of the women wanted to know about me, who I was. They were very impressed my dad was Chinese because your lineage goes through your father and your identity goes through your father. So it was good that my father was Chinese because then that was a big deal, that was very honorable, and so I was pretty well-known among the Vietnamese.

Cu Chi was out in the middle of nowhere. It was near Nui Ba Den, the Black Virgin Mountain. There was a lot of fighting up there. There was a lot of fighting around us. It was the VC's stronghold and it still is a Communist stronghold. Communists live there, very political, high-class Communists are still in that area, so it has a history of being Communist controlled. The base was large, not as large as Long Binh, but it had its own airport, and mostly for the Jolly Green Giant helicopters and the Chinooks, but not jet planes. C-130s—supply planes— would go in there. It was a very large base. We had everything from engineers to finance. We had the whole nine yards there. And we were surrounded by VC country. It was dry during dry season, dry enough where people couldn't wear contact lenses because it would scratch their eyes. The sand would get in between the lens and the eyes. It was like desert, and then when it rained during monsoon season it was wet. The hospital would be flooded up to our knees with water and, of course, roofs would be leaking. Most of the buildings were Quonset huts with a lot of holes in the roof. Of course the military didn't fix them, so we always had buckets all over the place during monsoon season.

The VC made their presence known. We were mortared on a regular basis. If we had POWs, they would try to hit us so that we wouldn't get information from them. Sometimes it would be quiet, nothing was going on, and other times it would just be mortars all night and casualties. Unfortunately, casualties and mortars go together. You're working twelve-, thirteen-, fourteen-hour days, you go home and you're exhausted, you just want to sleep, and you're getting mortared. I just refused to get out of my bed. I was just so tired and disgusted with the whole thing. It was like, "Come get me and kill me or just leave me alone, but you're not going to get me out of this bed. I'm not going to go underneath the bed where there's rats and roaches and stuff. I'm not going in the bunkers where there's rats and roaches, no, no. I'm just going to sleep in my bed and if you're going to get me, you're going to get me." So I really had a bad attitude about the whole thing, and what I remember about mortar attacks is just, "Fuck you, come get me." Sometimes I felt that if they killed me they would be doing me a favor because I was so tired and then I wouldn't have to deal with all this crap again. In some ways I was almost asking for it. I'd wake up in the morning and feel my body and say, "Yes, my physical body is still here," and sometimes I wasn't sure if I was happy that I was alive because I had to go back there to the hospital again and do this all over again. You get to be very hard-core.

The triage is like an emergency room, except it's like getting a train wreck. We called some people train wrecks where they were so fucked up that from head to toe it's like, where do you start? Triage is where we got the guys straight from the field, straight from the chopper, the evac, and they'd come in three to five at a time. Our triage was to separate, so as soon as you get somebody that's got simple wounds you send them out to lie on a board. The docs are usually there, the surgeons are usually there, and they decide, "Okay, this one, this one, this one's got to go to surgery right now." Then there's others that are just so messed up that it's not like they're not worth taking care of, it's just that they would take so much time that maybe three would die while we were taking care of one. So the decision is that we have to let that one die because he'll probably die within a few minutes anyway. We don't have the time or the staff to try and save them, versus other people that were severely wounded but have a pretty good chance of making it through the operating room. We just had an understanding among ourselves that the guys that would be set to the side to die, that they wouldn't die alone. We refused to allow that. A lot of times you were expected to just let them die and take care of whoever needs taking care of, but as long as there was one or two people working on an injured person, I felt that was enough for me to be with somebody who was dying, because a lot of us didn't believe that anybody should die alone.

It was so important because if I was dying I would want somebody to be there with me. It's a very spiritual experience for me as a nurse and for my dying patient. All kinds of intimate things happen. Intimate. The conversation is very intimate. A lot of them kept on telling me they would be okay. A lot of them would ask me if I was okay. That's how they would start the conversation, "Are you okay?" And I'd think, "Yeah, I'm okay, are you okay?" They would talk about their wives, they'd talk about their children, most of the time they talked about their mothers. They knew that their mothers would suffer a great deal. They were very concerned about that, and I would just listen. I really didn't know how to deal with this. I dealt with sixty-five-year-old men dying of heart attacks or having strokes, people dying of cancer, and you knew this was happening and you were trying to give them comfort. But what do you do with a nineteen-year-old boy who's like a younger brother, who's going to leave the planet, who's concerned about his mother, concerned about his wife, concerned about his child, and all I could do is be there with him? I got a sense of peace from them and I understand it more now than I did then. At that time I was young. I didn't have mentors to help me deal with the dying process. I had to deal with it all by myself, but I did get a great sense of comfort and peace after they died. I didn't understand that. It wasn't until many years later, when I met Elizabeth Kubler Ross, a famous psychiatrist who worked with dying people. We talked about the dying process and what happens. I got comfort from her when I talked to her about this and her telling me, "You did everything right."

I felt it was important to be with somebody who was dying. Especially these young boys. Sometimes they would say, "Don't leave me, don't leave me," and I wouldn't do that. I do know that there's a story of a nurse that did and when she came back he had died and she felt terribly guilty about that. I think I had an inner sense that this was just as important as taking care of the living and trying to save them. I got a lot of peace from it and I was very confused about that. I didn't grieve so much for them, because remember, once he died, my job was to go back to the living again. I didn't really have time to grieve. I didn't have time to contemplate what had happened. My job was to go to the next patient, get myself back to saving people who were clinging to life. I practice Buddhism now. A lot of us do. I thought I was so unique but the more Vietnam vets I run into the more I realize that this is a pretty common journey for us. There is a famous Buddhist teacher, Thich Non Hon, who is a Vietnamese monk who came to the United

States and pleaded with our government not to get involved in the Vietnam War, that it really wasn't our place. Dr. King nominated him for a Nobel Peace Prize. He comes back to the United States every so many years. He lives in France. He's not allowed to go back to his country because he's considered a traitor and he meets with Vietnam vets to talk about war and the suffering and recovering.

There's damage, but there's also a growth. These men would never have done well if they lived. I see these triple amps that did make it and I wonder how difficult their lives are. Some of them are married to these wonderful women, have families, and others are not doing that well. There was one that killed himself. He was a marine named Lewis Puller, a triple amp, who ended up drinking, couldn't fight the bottle, and killed himself. That affected me greatly because he had come all this way and he did this to himself and he was married and had children, and he did this to himself. But I can't even imagine what it's like to live that way. So in some ways, it was a blessing. In other ways, some of these triple amps that are rolling around in their wheelchairs remind people of the cost of war and that's good. It's good that people are reminded about this.

I have spent the past thirty years seeking spiritual and psychological recovery, and I seek it all the time, and in a way it's a blessing because this is something I have to do inside me. For some other people it may be a choice, a nice thing to follow a spiritual path. For me, it's a necessity to survive, to keep on going day by day, to justify all that stuff that happened. I think my job is to teach our society about war, because when people get all excited about going to the Persian Gulf and going here and going there, no one's thinking about the price, not only of the person that's going but the price of the family. One of my worst nightmares was being drafted again, being sent back to

Vietnam, being sent back to the war and crying, just grieving, and telling the government I have these children, you can't take me away from my children. That was the worst nightmare I had. During the Persian Gulf War the worst nightmare was in the media. I saw this one navy nurse on a ship signing—her daughter was deaf—signing to her deaf daughter, "I love you." I thought, "Oh my God, my worst nightmare is here, how could they do this?" Yes, women need to be in the military, but when they have children, or when they have little children.... There was a story during the Gulf War of a couple that left their infant behind. Both were in the military, and they had to leave the child with a foster family. This is nuts. People cheering away, "Oh yes, we're going to the Persian Gulf, we're going to save our little oil fields," and that's how I see it, blood for oil. I didn't join the protesters, but I wasn't upset that they were there, because I thought, "Yeah, blood for oil. What's wrong with this country? Are we so self-centered that all we care about is our own comfort?" It's not even comfort, our own luxury, allowing other people to suffer for our luxury, and that's what I see in Kosovo right now, and Bosnia.

Everybody was against the Wall because it was this ugly thing in the earth. But the more I learned about the memorial, that there'd be names on there, the more I felt it was something that was appropriate for our war. At the time, the VA had hired me to go back there to talk about the women veterans. I was on a committee and they took us to the memorial before it was finished. They had some of the slabs in piles and some of them were already what would be the Wall. I'm an observer and I am watching everybody touching the names on the Wall, and even touching the names on the slabs and I thought, "Wow, this is very interesting, because I can't keep my hands off of it either, there's something very tactile about this." So I went back for the dedication and people were all over the Wall. Everybody was touching the Wall. The names were so significant. It wasn't a big giant statue where you're diverted from what it's all about, you're honing in on what this memorial is about. It's about names, it's about people who lost their lives, or people who are missing in action.

I had stopped and talked to a number of guys and I told them that I was an army nurse in Vietnam, and before I knew it, all these men wanted to hug me and thank me and tell me stories and that was the beginning of my healing process, because I was getting acknowledged for what went on over there. I thought because I was a woman I wasn't very significant or very important in the war. I hadn't realized how important we were, and I hadn't realized it wasn't just because we were nurses, it was because we were women, because we were over there. Even when we were off duty, we would be stopped, and men would stop and talk to us, like the guys from New York or the Northeast wanting to hear this accent. We were like the girls next door. We were very significant, not just as nurses but as women. That's when I became more in touch with my femininity. It was something appreciated by men. All this sex objectivity that I experienced stateside wasn't really what I was experiencing in Vietnam. I was experiencing the appreciation of being a woman. Men would say to me that I smelled good, that I looked soft, "Could you just stand here and talk to me? I've not been around an American woman in a long time and it just feels good to stand here and talk to you." I started to appreciate myself more as a woman than I had before then, and I have to give them the credit for putting down their macho stuff that men do and just be human beings and say, "I appreciate you for being a woman, I appreciate you being here, I appreciate your femininity, I appreciate who you are as a woman," and so I was getting this at the Wall. The guys were coming up and saying wonderful things about us, and of course all the speech-makers who were talking about gentlemen and servicemen never mentioned women. Then there was a general that got up, and he said, "I want to thank both the men and the women, and if you're near any nurse, you need to go up to her and give her a hug for what she's done for you in Vietnam." And before I knew it, men were lined up hugging. There was about six of us that had found each other. They were lining up wanting to give us hugs, and saying, "Thank you, you know, we really appreciate you." Men coming up to me crying and telling me they never got the chance to thank their nurse and I became their substitute nurse, so to speak. I realized that we were greatly appreciated. Maybe this country didn't appreciate us, but the people that were the most important to me were the Vietnam vets. They appreciated what we did, and that's what was so significant. Then in 1990, about eight years later, I ended up working for the Department of Veteran Affairs and counseling Vietnam vets. Still healing.

At the tenth anniversary of the dedication of the Wall, in 1992, there was a display of a memorial to the women vets, Vietnam vets, that we wanted to erect by the Wall. The women were saying, "Oh, you need to see it, you need to see it," so we all went over there to see it. The men had put flowers around it. They had put twenty dollar bills, one hundred dollar bills, around the table. Men were crying. We were crying, because again, you forget how much you're appreciated by these men and then you see they wanted this statue to be erected for us, and they were going to put money there, they were handing us checks. In the middle of all this, I heard this one guy say, "Lily, are you Lily?" I turn around and it was Jim, Jim Fleck, and he said, "You remember me?" I thought, "No, not really," and he described that he had been hit and had a head concussion and that he was in the ICU that I worked at. I said, "Well, I don't know." I said, "Nobody knew my first name." He said, "Don't you remember, I bothered you, I bothered you for a long time trying to get you to tell me your name, your first name and you made me promise not to call you by your first name during day shift, because I'd get in trouble, and that night shift it was okay." Then I remembered, and he said, "I thought it was you, but I wasn't sure, but then I heard your voice and I knew it was you because I remembered your voice." It was just so neat to run into somebody who remembered me and appreciated what I did. I didn't do a whole lot, not for him, not really, but to see that he was okay and he was doing well and he was a fire-fighter in Massachusetts and that he was living a happy life.

When I got back, I learned real quick not to talk about the war. It was a very alone feeling, because I didn't go back with other vets. I didn't hang out with other vets. Although I was looking for them, I had no idea of where to go. It was very lonely for about twelve years until the vet centers started to provide counseling for Vietnam vets. They were like out-patient clinics under the VA. That's when I found out that all that I had gone through was post–traumatic stress, that I had post–traumatic stress disorder. Then there was also an organization called Vietnam Veterans of America which I got very involved in. That and the clinic was also a place to meet other vets.

The thing I remember is the children in Vietnam. The children were in despair. There weren't too many happy children, but I went back in 1995 with a group of women vets and the children are not in despair, they're just normal, happy every-day children. There aren't limbs missing. I'm quite sure there are in some parts of the country, but overall, the country is healing, has healed, and the children haven't a clue what war is all about. I'm very thankful for that because in my time all the children were affected by war, and that affects me the most. Even now in our modern times, I think of the children, and how it will affect them for the rest of their lives.

Lily Jean Adams was born in New York and lived in Manhattan, Queens, and Yonkers. She graduated from Lincoln High School in Yonkers and from the Mt. Vernon Hospital School of Nursing. After Vietnam she returned to nursing, working in Houston as an open heart surgery specialist and in San Francisco as a float nurse. She earned a Bachelor of

Arts in psychology and her Master's in developmental psychology, both at San Francisco State University. In 1980 she joined the Vietnam Veterans of America and helped start chapters in Honolulu, Atlanta, and Marin County. She stayed deeply involved with Vietnam and worked for the Veteran's Administration for eight years as a PTSD counselor. Recently she coordinated a study on Asian-American Vietnam veterans. She speaks at universities and veterans and professional groups, and is Assistant Clinical Professor, School of Nursing, University of California, San Francisco. Adams is the mother of a twenty-five-year-old daughter and a twenty-one-year-old son. She says, "I am presently taking a break from the world and focusing on myself and my own much-needed healing. I'm burnt out. I have incorporated meditation and tai chi into my mornings, working out in the gym regularly and focusing on my spirituality."

JACKIE KNOLL
AIR FORCE FLIGHT NURSE

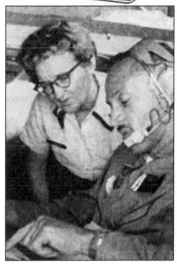

A career officer in the air force, Jackie Knoll was a part of the 57th Air Medical Evacuation Squadron based in Clark Field, the Philippines. From 1969 to 1971, she was often on the huge C-141A transport planes, equipped as flying hospitals, that flew into South Vietnam empty and carried the wounded back to safety. In Vietnam, airbuses on the ground loaded with wounded soldiers would drive up the rear of the airplane. There, they discharged the wounded men to the waiting nurses who cared for them on their long journey. Sometimes, though, Knoll stayed in Vietnam for a week before flying out with wounded troops. She and the other flight nurses were usually in the air and, like their sisters on the ground, they rarely got any sleep.

I had been in the air force for a few years and I already had career status as a nurse. Other nurses were going to Vietnam, whether they had been in for several years or were recently in service. Other friends that had been in for longer periods of time were going and it was just a matter of time until I would be going and I wanted to get it over with, so I volunteered to go. That was the writing on the wall.

Getting on the plane to go I was excited, afraid, and all else at once. I wasn't going directly to Vietnam. I was going to have a stop-over in Hawaii on the way for mainly classroom-type survival training with flight crews on other types of planes. It was just for a few days. In flight nursing school we had some classes on survival in case the plane went down over water with all the patients. You learned how you would try to save the patients and yourself. We practiced jumping into a raft from a plane mock-up. The Hickham Air Force Base classes ended with that and how to use emergency items for survival.

In Vietnam we had three temporary quarters located at Danang, Cam Ranh Bay, and Tan Son Nhut Air Base, which is near Saigon. We flew air evacuation of wounded guys on a C-141A cargo jet that was converted for that purpose. The plane I was on flew into combat areas. The North Vietnamese seemed to know our medical evacuation schedules and that we had wounded patients aboard and fired at our planes at times. We flew into Vietnam empty from Clark Air Force Base, the Philippine Islands, and we were combined with Yakota Air Base, Japan Air Evacuation squadron. The three bases I just mentioned were pickup points. Patients were brought there within twenty-four hours of departure. Usually two or three regularly scheduled flights went to two of the three bases to pick up patients daily. Sometimes more planes had to be added when fighting and wounded were heavier than usual. We'd leave Clark Air Force Base at night. Usually the first flights would leave around maybe 11 P.M. and then the others would be a few hours later. There might be up to three planes that were scheduled into some of the places, and we would fly in empty with our medical crew. The team was made up of two nurses and three medical flight techs or corpsmen with extra training from a special school. There were no doctors on board our flights.

Our planes didn't go out in the field and pick up wounded patients because our plane was much too large for that. Others brought our patients to the pick-up points in ambulances. Some patients were on ships. Some patients, because they were in such poor physical condition, were brought directly to the planes by Dustoff or other choppers and they arrived a short time before takeoff.

Many patients were very badly injured. They had head wounds and some of them had had surgery. Usually their wounds were not just in one place. When a man was hit by ammunition, it usually involved several areas like organs, bones, muscles, blood vessels, and everything else. It was never a nice, clean, small incision as doctors make when doing surgery on just one organ, but tears and cuts and any and all types of trauma. They were badly torn up. Others were paralyzed. We had patients with limbs off. Many patients were unconscious or comatose.

When we arrived our medical crews got off the plane and met with those of ours working on the ground in planning and preparing for the air evacuation flights. They gave us a report on the patients we would be carrying. During this time the hospital medical evacuation casualty staging unit took the patients to the plane and boarded them in pre-arranged spaces preparing them for takeoff. Our flight crew rechecked the patients, saw if they needed anything for pain and gave them pain meds. We did any other necessary tasks such as checking the medical equipment attached to the men. The transfer from the ground facility was not very easy for the patients. They had tubes from everywhere. They had equipment for intravenous fluids, tubes from the urinary bladder, and the chest, and the abdomen, and through the nose, and into the stomach or intestines, for example. They had casts. Some had breathing equipment, respiratory equipment, and Byrd machines were mostly used then, but other types of respiratory equipment were being tested to see if they performed better in flight. We also had large Styker frames that were mainly for paralyzed patients. The man was held in place on a board with a soft cover and when he was turned, he was sandwiched between two similar frames. This equipment was very large and heavy and took up a great amount of space.

Nineteen was the average age of these wounded guys. I remember one young guy, probably twenty years old. These guys had gone to Vietnam in good physical condition and now this young man was torn up pretty badly. Usually their small air evac record only named one of several injuries each patient had. I believe it said abdominal wounds, but there were really many others. He had a foot missing, too. Most guys didn't let you know or see them cry, but this guy did cry openly a lot of times during this long flight. He was in pain off and on and I gave him medication as often as I could. I know that he was worried about going back and facing family, friends, and those who were used to him as he was before. He worried that he might not be accepted by others. He also worried about how much longer he would have to have medical care and how he would be when it ended. That's the usual thing. They had a lot of other fears. They knew about the protesting going on back in the U.S. against the war and that it was sometimes directed at them for being there. That was scary.

We sometimes came under fire on the planes, but not always. They always had us in their sights, especially on take-off. They didn't care that we were picking up patients. One of our C-141s was hit by a very large rocket on takeoff with all of the patients on board. It knocked out most of the navigation equipment but fortunately it was a dud and it didn't explode. They had to return to base, off-load the patients, and then remove the rocket. If that thing had exploded, no one would have lived.

We were under fire on the ground at times, especially when we were working ground duty as in the planning and preparation of the air evac flights. The noises were very loud—big booms. You saw different lights. Some of the booms were ours and others were incoming.

Another flight nurse and I were doing ground duty at Tan Son Nhut one time and there was shelling during the night. We had bunk beds and two of us were in a room. The other nurse was on the top bunk and under fluorescent lights. She was afraid that if a rocket hit, it would shatter that bulb on her and she would be all cut up. We were both very tired as we had been working most of the last twenty-four hours with only short times for naps or just rest. We had just gotten to our room a while before the shelling started and we knew we had to be up and working in another few hours. You couldn't get any sleep with all the noise from the rockets exploding. We talked about what we should do to try to be safe. We had the lights off, but she was afraid that they would break on her and there was nothing to keep the pieces from falling down on her. We knew there was a bunker in the area and we were really supposed to go there but we were afraid we might not find it in the dark. But I don't think I wanted to go. If we did get into it, there might be poisonous snakes inside and we would be no better off than in our room. She decided to try to get under my lower bunk in case the light bulbs broke but there wasn't enough room there. She ended up sleeping on the floor under a small table and felt safer. I was able to get some sleep off and on in between the noise and all. They did hit an ammunition dump there that night but we lucked out except for some sleep.

In Danang, there was a lot of incoming, quite often. Once we had just come from working at the air evac hospital there and we had to walk between the hospital and the corpsmen's barracks to our own administration section to finish our work and leave. A short time later, incoming started and we were told that the corpsmen's barracks had been hit. Several guys were having a short-timer's party for those leaving in a few hours to about a week. Several of them were killed or injured. This was unfortunately part of life in Vietnam.

One time we were returning back from the states, or dead-heading, without patients. We were going back to pick up more and start all over again. We called it a yo-yo flight. When we got to Japan we caught a daily flight for returning medical air evac crews that took us to Clark. Since we had very little sleep most of the time, I napped while waiting for maintenance. We really didn't get too awfully much sleep, so every time they would tell us to go somewhere and sit and wait, well, I'd fall asleep. We were being moved to various places to wait, such as on a bus or the air evac staging unit or even on the plane at times. We were finally on the plane and it took off. It was probably around 9 P.M. Japan time and our plane was scheduled to leave much earlier in the day. I fell asleep before takeoff and the next thing I'm wakened by being hit on the chest by the engineer going down the aisles and yelling that we were going down. I asked the nurse sitting next to me if we were really going down and she said the plane had been out of control since we took off and yes, something's wrong. She said, "They've been trying to turn around and go down." I started praying a lot. I knew that there was a mountain not too far away, Mt. Fuji, and so we were concerned, but there was nothing you could do really, but pray, that's about it. You couldn't get up out of your seat and run around or anything, so you sat there and worried a lot. A very young-looking pilot and the engineer were going to the back of the plane to look out and see if they could find the problem. I said, "Oh my gosh, that guy was so young, he'll never find what's wrong," but that guy did. I was wrong and we continued flying to Clark. Two fighter planes were sent to accompany us in case we had further problems. That way they would have seen our location and passed it on for the search-and-rescue teams if we had gone down during the flight. It was a very scary time and we were all very happy to get on the ground again.

We stopped at most military bases with larger hospitals and exchanged patients from the Far East to the United States and within the United States. We had two main routes—the northern and southern Pacific routes. The northern route was from Japan through Alaska and into Illinois and onto the East Coast and sometimes Andrews Air Force Base, Maryland, and back to McGuire Air Force Base, New Jersey, and spend the night or what was left of it. The southern route was from the Philippines through Guam and sometimes Wake and Hawaii and into California. Sometimes we were extended south to San Diego or north to Washington State or east to Kelly Air Force Base, Texas, near San Antonio. Then we flew back to California to spend the night whether much was left or not.

When I got to the Far East it was during Tet of 1969 and it was very busy. We carried an average load of sixty or more patients. Most were on canvas stretchers and were tiered or placed on top of each other, with very little space between and three or four patients high. There was six or so inches between each canvas stretcher. Two rows were in the center, separated by a sheet for some privacy. There was a narrow aisle on each side of the two rows and another row was against the fuselage. Other patients were ambulatory or sitting in passenger seats. We kept a few empty stretchers because some of these guys weren't as strong as they thought and had to be put on a stretcher for the rest of the flight.

There was another whole air evac outfit that went out into the boonies. There were choppers that went out there to pick up guys. They brought them to pickup points or exchanged them in the Far East. They sometimes had North Vietnamese prisoners or Vietnamese families or even pigs or chickens on planes with our wounded guys. Sometimes that was about all the Vietnamese had and they would not part with them.

For me, probably within a twenty-four-hour period there could have been two or three separate loads. There would be one whole plane load and then we would change patients, so probably 150 or so, I imagine, by the time you switched patients around on some of the legs that we were on. It was very depressing when you thought too much about it, about what you were seeing, to think about these young guys and their wounds and all the medical treatment they would have to have. Many would be in wheelchairs the rest of their lives. When you were taking care of them, it helped you and them to be able to talk and listen to them if and when you had the time.

When they came on board they were usually pretty happy to be going back with us. The pilot announced when we were leaving Vietnam air space and there was a lot of cheering. Many of the guys talked to each other and were in pretty good spirits until we left Japan for the United States. The closer we got to the states, the quieter it was. Most didn't seem as happy as before. It was the same as I mentioned before with the badly wounded guy. They were afraid of not being accepted and were mainly afraid of the protesters.

I was already older in age than many other nurses who were there and I aged even more in those two years. It was a learning experience about people and wars and most life situations. I learned a lot more about people and thought a little bit more about people and all and what all happens to them. I really never expected to be in a wartime situation in my lifetime, and it was traumatic. It was something you could only find in war. It was not in nice clean hospitals in the U.S.

I would avoid it at all costs now, and if I had it to do over again I would say that I would, but having had that experience, it's the most memorable of all my tours and all the places I worked. I'll never forget it. It was because of the guys, the young guys, and how badly injured they were. I was doing more in the way of nursing than anywhere else. At first it was kind of a shock because in the states we were used to taking care of the kids and the wives when they delivered their babies and the guys in nice, clean hospitals. But not guys with the war wounds these patients had. Most guys we carried were injured pretty badly. Air evac over long distances on the planes and caring for wounded patients was very different. The hours were much longer and there wasn't much time off. The duty was much more independent than in most nursing jobs at the time. It wasn't nearly as clean as most hospitals. If you ran out of supplies there was no way of getting more on the flight. You had to figure out other ways of using and making do with what you had on hand. Our working space was much more confined than in a hospital. Sometimes you had to do some climbing around to see equipment or casts or a patient's skin color and much more. Sometimes you had to crawl under the lower stretchers to see similar things as those on the higher levels. You did what you had to do for the patients' care. I felt that I was using my nursing experience for more of what it was intended than at any other time in that profession.

There were lots of casts, lots of limbs off, lots of bad injuries, just really bad. Like I said, there were several bad things wrong with them. Not just a little hole somewhere that a surgeon would make or something like that at all. They blew up inside and it went out the back. Usually the entrance hole wasn't as bad, but the exit hole was very bad and very bad inside. It took their lives.

On the flight, it was like being in a hospital ward, sort of, except that you were in much more confined quarters and you were limited. We had no doctors on board. We knew about how long we were going to be flying. Some flights were very long. Between Japan and Travis Air Force Base in California was probably our longest, and depending on the weather and wind and a lot of things, it was ten hours, and so you had all that time to take care of them. But other flights were very short, say between two different places in Vietnam when you're practically just up and down and you were just taking patients on. Maybe you picked up half of a load at one place and half of a load at another. Usually the next stop was Japan and that was a few more hours.

I was very fortunate that no patients ever died on any of my flights. In thinking of numbers, deaths on air evac flights are very low. I don't know why they didn't die because there were a lot that were bad enough to have died at any time. Sometimes there was a death on some of the flights. It's around 1 percent.

Any are too many, but we worked to keep all the badly wounded patients alive and getting them safely to their final medical facility.

Our teams usually worked together more than in the states. There were lots of people along the way that these guys had taking care of them, and no one person can ever take credit for anything. We did all we could for the patients to get them home and get them into good care.

We did a lot of flying during that time. Usually I wasn't afraid to fly and I did like it, but some of my friends were afraid of flying but tried to be brave for their careers.

When I came home most people had no interest in anything about Vietnam, especially from those of us who were there. I remember someone in the service in the United States that did ask me about Vietnam but didn't like what I said. He told me he watched TV every night and saw what was going on in Vietnam and it was nothing like what I said. Being back home and working at a military hospital was a different experience than before I left. I was stationed in Northern California in an area where there was a lot of protesting going on and even outside the gate. I learned not to wear my uniform anywhere off base and to have other clothes over it when driving to and from work off base. I had my car on base. I worked evenings and one evening coming off duty I went out to my car to find the headlights knocked out. Other nurses had missing batteries.

After working all night I had an early morning appointment for X-rays. I had my white uniform on and had to change into an X-ray gown and leave my uniform in the dressing room. All the others had been taken ahead of me and I was told to reschedule my appointment because they were finished for the day. I told them I had been there all morning and I spoke to the radiologist. He agreed to do my tests after lunch. When I went back to the dressing room I found my new white uniform ruined. Someone had put gum, that had been chewed, of course, inside the uniform and wadded up the uniform, then stepped all over it. They seemed to have repeated it several times. The uniform was completely ruined.

We have eight female names that are on the Vietnam Memorial, the Wall, and one was in the air force and worked on the same medical air evacuation staging unit as I did. She was new in the air force and worked in various hospitals for a few years and then flew air evac. She was killed, along with many civilian women, on the C-5A Operation Babylift crash near Saigon in April of 1975.

I think that we need to think about the women. Of course that's very few in comparison to the guys but I think the guys are pretty good. I think that they've been made a lot more aware. The guys have helped us get our statue, the Vietnam Women's Memorial near the Wall in Washington, D.C. We wouldn't have had it without the guys' help.

Some people realize that women were in Vietnam. A few of them at the Wall will say different things. Some of them don't realize that there were women, and don't realize women were there. There is no real way of counting the military women in Vietnam because we found out later that instead of having an "F" for female, we all had an "M" for male on our records. So women weren't there. Our government usually denied having females in Vietnam. If there's no "F" for females over there, then I guess there weren't any females there, at least that was the attitude back then. I didn't realize it until I had to go for a records check. I thought that it was a typing error at the time, not unusual, but I found out later that it was on purpose.

Back then it was, it was nothing to have someone walk away from you when you tell them you're a Vietnam vet. Now I think it's a little more open and people want to know a little bit more about it. What were you doing there? Why were you there? Just guys there? I think people are curious and want to know why women were there and what they did.

Jackie Knoll was born and brought up in the small town of Harmon, Illinois. The daughter and granddaughter of farmers, she attended two years of high school in Harmon until the school closed. She then went to live with her grandparents in Hollywood, Florida, in 1950 and there she completed high school. Her biggest thrill at the time was being in the concert and marching band, playing at all the events and having the

time of her life. She first enlisted in the air force in 1955 and resigned in 1957, when she decided she wanted to be a nurse. Trained at the Copley Memorial Hospital School of Nursing in Aurora, Illinois, she graduated in 1960. She rejoined the air force in 1962 with a commission of 2nd Lieutenant. Knoll was with the air force in France from 1963 to 1966, and then returned home to Vandenberg Air Force Base. By 1969 she was a captain based at Clark Field, the Philippines. Her assignment was as a flight nurse ferrying wounded from Vietnam battlefields to hospitals in the United States, the Philippines, or Japan. After returning to the states, she earned a degree from Chapman University. She retired from the air force as major in 1979, and until recently, Knoll and her cat Rascal roamed around the country in her RV. She teaches basic literacy classes, and does volunteer work with the Vietnam Veterans of America, including helping run soup kitchens. She enjoys playing cards and board games, and going to movies. She has collected money for The Salvation Army on holidays and collects money for Vietnam veterans organizations. Jackie Knoll is proudest of the work she does with the Traveling Wall, sponsored by the Vietnam Veterans of America, which continuously tours the country. A smaller replica of the Wall in Washington, it gives people a sense of what the real Wall is for those who never get a chance to see it.

ELIZABETH ALLEN
ARMY NURSE

Elizabeth Allen was twenty-six years of age in 1967 when she arrived in Vietnam with her Master's degree in psychiatric nursing and business administration. Commissioned a captain, her first assignment was in Cu Chi, the headquarters for the 25th Division situated between the Cambo-

dian border and Saigon. She served at the 71st Evacuation Hospital in Pleiku during the brutal November 1967 battle between the 173rd Airborne and North Vietnamese for Hill 875 in Dak To. Her nursing was hard-core nursing, including medical evacuation flights on helicopters and assignments running triage. She says, "It's an experience that I'm not sure I would want to do again, but I would do again if called upon to do it . . . if that makes sense. That's just me."

I had just finished my Master's program at Ohio State and I went to Vietnam in 1967. The war was gearing up, and I had two brothers that were in the war. My older brother and I were

83

both in Vietnam at the same time, even though they said that couldn't be done. He was in the navy and I was in the army. I knew that I didn't want to continue to do what I was doing, and I had been a nurse for a long time, and one day I decided that I was going to go to Vietnam. I knew that there were very few African American health professionals in Vietnam. They just weren't there, period. I also knew that there were a lot of frontline African American troops, and they needed some-body, too. The guys would say to me a lot of times, "I came to see you, to let me know what I'm fighting for," because other-wise it wasn't for them.

I signed up for the air force first. With the Master's degree and long-time experience, I would be commissioned captain. The air force nurse that I interviewed with, a lieutenant, did not like the fact that I was going to come in ahead of her, and so the paperwork was slow. One day I went to the army and I talked to the army and I told them I'll go with whichever one gets me in first and gets me to Vietnam. The army picked me up at home, picked me up at work, and the air force sent it to my home, that's how I got in the army as opposed to being in the air force. My deal with them, was that I would go straight to Vietnam. I did not owe the military anything, and I had a Mas-ter's degree, my ticket was safe. The army agreed to send me to the next class and before I filled out any papers even, they got me a guaranteed assignment to Vietnam. When I went to OCS, they tried to change me and wanted to send me to the Univer-sity of Maryland and I fought that. I wanted to go to Vietnam, that was our agreement. The army wanted me to teach because I was already Master's prepared, and I didn't want to do that. I could teach anywhere.

Then they gave me an assignment to Fitzsimmons, which everybody wanted because it was in the Rockies. I didn't want to go to Fitzsimmons, so they changed it, and then I got to go to Vietnam. When I got there, of course, I was the ranking person coming in country, so I got to pick where I wanted to go. They wanted me in Saigon, which had the white uniforms and the nurses hats. It wasn't for me, and somebody real smart says, well why don't you send her to Cu Chi? I really didn't know anything about it. Colonel Strader, she was such a lady, she said, "You don't want to go to Cu Chi." I said, "Why don't I want to go to Cu Chi?" She says, "They've just taken the tent tops off and it is close to the Black Virgin Mountain, it is in the middle of the battle, and it is with the 25th Infantry Division." I said, " I'll take it," and she said, "You have got to be kidding." I said, "I'll take it."

I get into country on a Thursday. I'm transferred to Cu Chi on Friday, and they're going to orient me to the battle on Monday. On Saturday we get hit. It was just me and one other person. I know nothing. I don't know where to go. I don't know where to run. The people who were there, they all start running to the bunkers. I don't know how to get to the bunkers. So finally somebody says, "Come on, follow us." Frankie and I run out to the bunkers, and we get in these bunkers, and the water, it's like up to your ankles. You're sitting around on these makeshift seat things, and I don't know what to do, so I'm sitting there with my feet down. Somebody says, "Get your feet up, there's snakes in the water." Well Jesus Christ—I don't know what to do. Then, when they let you out of the bunkers, you got to go back to work, and that's a very, very difficult thing to do day after day.

My first real experience and I think what really caught me, was when we went outside. There were a lot of young troops sitting around, a lot of young boys sitting around, just leaning on their duffel bags. There was a sergeant walking with me and

I said to him, "Why are they sitting there like that?" He said, "They're waiting for somebody to come for them." I said, "How long do they have to wait?" He said, "Until somebody needs them." I said, "What does that mean?" He said, "They are replacement troops." I said, "I don't understand." He said, "They come in and they wait for a unit assignment." I said, "Let's go over this. Are you telling me that all of these guys— there were thousands of them just sitting—that when somebody gets killed or injured, that company comes in and picks up how many they need?" He said, "That's exactly right." I said, "So they're waiting for somebody to get killed." He said, "That's right." I said, "Do they know that?" He said, "It don't matter." Like how does an eighteen-year-old wait for somebody to die? That was really hard for me, and it was an impression that stayed with me throughout the whole time. There are battle units that come in and pick these youngsters up and take them, and it rotates.

My routine was different depending upon the battle that surrounds you. My first duty, and this was probably one of my more interesting ones, and one that a lot of people didn't have, was I worked solely with Vietnamese. They didn't know where to put me because I did have a Master's degree. That was kind of uncomfortable for the unit, so I worked on a Vietnamese unit. There were a lot of bus bombings. We got a lot of civilians with a lot of strange kinds of diseases, plague, injuries that were totally foreign to us. We got one guy that had an abdominal injury, and they had cut him open and stuffed it with straw. We had to do something to get that straw out. The bus bombing are mine injuries, legs off and arms off. They didn't have the prosthetic kinds of things to fix. A lot of hunger, food poisonings, difficult deliveries. If GI groups came upon them, they would bring me in.

Once a week we would go out on a med caps, which are medical missions, to work in the field with the Vietnamese. That was very difficult because I didn't understand the language, I didn't understand the diseases that they had, and there was a lot that I had to learn. Plus you had to deal with the anger towards us, because Vietnamese troops also went to this unit. There was a lot of confusion on my part about how many of these Vietnamese soldiers do I give my all to, when I know that these are the same ones that create problems here? How do you make the philosophical decisions that you have to make? Remember, all South Vietnamese soldiers were not on the U.S. side. Viet Cong were South Vietnamese soldiers. North Vietnamese soldiers were in the NVA. You had the Viet Cong and the NVA, and a lot of confusion because they all looked alike. Not that their faces were all alike, but they were all basically from the same culture, same size, same general characteristics, and so it was very difficult to know how many were spies, how many were infiltration. We had the same problem with the children. We had a lot of children around the camps and U.S. soldiers will adopt anybody and anything, and so you didn't know if these kids' brothers were Viet Cong or if they were Viet Cong or if the girls were Viet Cong and so there was a lot of confusion in your mind about what to do.

The hospital was different from World War II and Korea. There was no front and no rear. Everybody keeps thinking that hospitals were always in the rear. There was no rear in Vietnam. As a matter of fact, the 25th Infantry Division base camp was built on top of the tunnels of Cu Chi, so the war was everywhere at the same time. The base camp could be blown up at any time, and battles were taking place on the base camp, the hospital was being hit by mortars and by rockets and you worked under those conditions all the time. *M.A.S.H.* makes it sound like everybody came in clean. That wasn't true. You knew when a maneuver was going on because the troops would all go out, and they would say, "Wolfhounds are going out tomorrow, both the 2nd and 25th, 26th, and 27th are all going out." You see them going out, so you knew that you had to rest, because you will have to work until the job is done. When they went out in the day, you knew how many were going to go and in the evening you saw how many gents are going to come back.

I've always been in psychiatry and there were things that I needed to know. I felt like I needed to know in order to be good at what I did. The 25th air cav, even though it's not connected to the 25th infantry division, is Airborne armor. They had the big tanks, and tank injuries are very different from grunt injuries. The guys who carry the M16s, these injuries were different. I made friends with the air cav. I had gone over and I rode on the tanks and I had been inside them. When a kid was in a tank injury, he had a lot of trouble if you put this full body cast on him because he'd already been in this can. He'd go crazy inside this full body cast. So, we had made arrangements that I was going to go out with the cav and just before it's time to go, they contact me and say I can't go. They said, we've been called in on an emergency maneuver. I go to work at 7:00 in the morning, and somebody says, "Liz, the air cav took it, got hit badly." I said, "What the hell do you mean?" They said, "They blew them away." So, my first patient was the sergeant that I was going to ride with. The bad part is he's a basket case. What's sad, he's got no arms and no legs, and I was going to ride with him. That was real hard, because I just saw him, and now he comes back, totally destroyed physically. You saw a lot of that, especially when you're in the base camp with them.

At Tet, you would see a kid and he maybe was guarding the perimeter and then he gets killed on the base camp and you get him back dead. That makes it really hard to separate what you see, or even to know what you actually saw.

One of the things that I think that keeps you healthy is to be able to sort things, because if my anticipation is that my friend is going to come back, then I put faces on them all, and I can't make the kind of decisions that I have to make. I have to sort that so I can do what I need to do. After I was six weeks on the Vietnamese unit, I went to surgical intensive care so that I got them after they came in from the OR. But that also meant that I was on unload and triage. The people in the operating room and the people in the recovery room got them first, then I got them, but they didn't waste any person power. When the choppers come in, everybody who's still there, who's not at a high intensity duty, has to unload the choppers, and, has to do triage, so I had to unload and do triage. In triage, the ones who were the least injured get treated first. If you've only got four operating rooms, and they're going to bring in 200 to 300 injured, you can't take four operating rooms and tie those up in twelve- or thirteen-hour surgeries. You've got to get them through there quick. You can't use all your blood supply on the most injured. The easier ones go first, and then you do your long-term ones, because that's the only thing that you can do. Now you have to deal with that, and so you can't get caught up with "this is my friend so I'm going to send him first."

You have to make those decisions, and they are difficult. What do you do when you run out of food, what do you do when you run out of medicine? We go crazy if a blood supply drops to thirty days, well, blood is gone, period. There is no gauze or bandages, and you do have to tear sheets. You do have to do that kind of thing. You have to work with what you've got, and when you're in the actual battle time, those are the kinds of decisions that you have to make.

I'm black. One of the things that the military has to do, and I don't fault them for this, but it's one of the things that you don't think about, is that there can be no fraternization between the officers and enlisted. There are very many enlisted African American men and there are very few African American officers. I'm an officer. I'm commissioned a captain. I've talked to some of my friends, and it was absolutely the loneliest time of my life, because there is nobody to go to, there's nobody to talk to, and that's true to this day. There is no one to go to, because people don't want to hear it. People want to catharsis about it, and they want to tie a yellow ribbon. They want to tell me about the experiences they had that they believed were the same, but nobody wants to hear what I have to say, because it's too painful for people to hear. I think that also accounts for why we see so many single women war veterans.

I went in as a twenty-six-year-old. The average age in Vietnam was nineteen. Most of the nurses who were there had been on the army nurse program, so they were twenty-one or twenty-two, or they were older women. There were a few African American women. It kind of set you apart. There were a very few where you were, because I mean, one time I was with two, one time I was with one, one time I was with none. You learn to keep your own counsel, and you get set apart. To this day, that has not changed.

Oh, there were good times. I did a lot of work with the troops. They even let me go to the enlisted clubs, and we'd get the women together and we would do line dances or round dances with them. One time, I remember one of the enlisted men touches me on the shoulder and I turned, and he said, "How would you like to have 900,090 Cokes, because everybody in here wants to buy you a Coke." It's that kind of thing. They would come in out of the field to talk to you. You could sit down and talk to them. When I needed things for the troops, it always worked for me, because many of your senior sergeants were black. We ran out of water and had nothing for them to drink. These were some tough times. I'd call over to special forces, and I'd call to transportation. I said, "Hey Sarg, I need something." He said, "What is it that you need now?" I said, "Fifteen cases of whatever you got to drink," and they would bring them to you, and the troops were real good in terms of doing things like that. You could always get a ride, you could always get a lift. I could ride in a deuce and a half, combat loaded. They'd scoot over and make a space for me, and we'd kind of laugh, and so there were a lot of really good times. Christmas was not as bad as people want to make it sound like it was. It was bad, you were away from home, but like the old song says, if you can't be with the one you love, love the one you're with, and the folks in the kitchen tried to make it as festive as they could make it. They tried to do the best they could, with whatever it was that they had. If I needed fatigues, I could call Sarg, even if I needed it for the troops in the field, I'd say, "Look, I need a whole box of fatigues." They'd find them for me and they would bring them in. They could help you learn how to do a whole lot with not very much, and you got good at it. I was a good nurse. I'm a damn good nurse. I still am, but I learned to make due with what I had. I think there were a lot of good times. I think that a lot of times when you had time off you could sit and you could talk because there were lulls in battle. It wasn't like the battle raged every day, all day.

There were times that you really did get to sit down. There were times that you got to read a magazine if you could get them. One of the funny things, and to this day when I tell my students about it they die laughing, is the military really doesn't make arrangements for women. One of the things was with the sanitary napkin. People don't think about this, and I always wonder why there were never any in any PX. One day I'm just kind of talking to Sarg, and I said, "Couldn't we just please get some tampons?" He looked at me and he said, "Well, we've been getting them." I said, "But they're not in the PX and they're not in any unit." One of the troops setting behind him said, "Are you talking about those cotton things with those strings on them?" I said, "Yeah, that's what I'm talking about." He said, "Well, we've been issuing those to the guys in the field." I said, "Come on, what are they using them for?" He said, "Those are the best things in the world to clean your piece with, your M16, because that little cotton pad fits right into the barrel and then that string, you just drop that down, you just pull that out and that's quick." I thought that was absolutely one of the funniest things I'd ever heard. They were sending them to us, but the guys were using them in the field. That was the best use for them, because they were quick, and as you probably know, the M16 was a machine that would jam quickly. One of the reasons was because of the dirt build-up and the oil build-up in them, so if they keep cleaning their weapon with them, they didn't have to worry about that anymore. They were being put to good use, but we laughed about that for the longest time—that the best cleaner for the M16 rifle was a tampon.

When I was at Cu Chi we had outhouses and the buckets, you know the cans. Sitting down was a real problem, and they used Agent Orange buckets. So there we were out there in the middle of the night, trying to go to the bathroom, and the hole was this far back from where your knees bent, so either you had to get up on top of the thing and stand there, or, you had to set there with your legal out. When you're doing that, the paper would drag on your behind, so there was a whole lot of problems with infection. The people were convinced that it was because the women were sexually active, rather than that it was the kind of facility that you had for a toilet.

For black women, there was a major hair problem. This was before the days of braids. There was no way to get your hair fixed. You can't press it, which is what black women do, because you've got to do it in the kitchen and most black women are not going to take care of their hair from white women. Where I was, we didn't have hot water. Because black women use oil in their hair, cold water doesn't move the hair, so there was no way to take care of your hair. There was no way to take care of your skin, and these were really very, very serious problems for African American women in the field. Laundry was a terrible problem, because you had to wring your clothing out, and in the monsoon hang them. You'd go to work in wet clothes, and you might spend three or four weeks in wet clothes. There was no way to get them dry and you had to wash them in the shower. They only give you three or six issues of clothes, so there was no way to get around that.

They heard that the troops were engaging in sex with the Vietnamese people, and so we needed to have something for them to do in their spare time. They sent ping-pong tables and volleyballs. That does not supplant sex in America, and it will not do it in the war zone, so I thought, "How naive can you be?" It's an art, ping-pong, but we laughed about that, because people, honest to God, do not realize that war is for real and people get hurt.

The American public really does not perceive the woman warrior, and I think that this is going to become a long-term problem, because now women are coming into combat groups.

The military is not set up to deal with that. To this day, as many veterans' hospitals that we have, we only have three women's units. These are relatively new units, and one of the major problems, and this may have been peculiar to Vietnam, so I want to separate that out, is that of the estimated number of women in Vietnam. I don't know why they don't know how many women were there. That blows me away.

During the Reagan administration they changed access rules to VA care, and category 4 would be any veteran who earns over $19,000 and does not have access to VA care. Guess what? All of those women earn more than that. Consequently, we do not have access to VA care. The long-term effect of that is that money is allocated based on the money you use. Since they were omitted by statute, there was no way that they could get back in, and people kept saying, "Well, there's nothing wrong with women, because we don't have any of them coming in." The reason they don't come in is because you omitted them by criterion. It's an awkward battle to try to get long-term care for women. Then, somebody made the decision that the only kind of problem that women would have would be rape, problems with rape, or OB/GYN, reproductive problems. The problems with cancer of the brain, the problems with cancer of the pancreas, the problems with post–traumatic stress, were never taken into account for women. The truth is, the rate of PTSD is higher in women than it is even in combat men. Even from the research angle, the estimates are so much higher for women, but there's no place for them to go.

All you saw was maimed eighteen-, nineteen-, twenty-year-olds. Twelve months of that can wear you down. Your whole time was in a traumatic situation, and you had to work under that trauma, so that you would be taking care of injured, at the same time you're being bombed, and you never had any weapon . . . never had a weapon. Like during Tet I was at Pleiku. We were surrounded. That morning you had discharged forty or fifty wounded. You couldn't keep them long because of a massive flow in, so you discharged those. I go back to work at 6:00 A.M. I had not left until 11 A.M. Just the magnitude of it, and the volume. I get thirty, forty admissions during the night. It's me, three corpsmen, and you're surrounded. You don't have a gun, and I'm responsible for all of these kids, all these troops, and there's no way out. They're petrified, you're petrified, the Geneva Convention precludes any weapon being on the unit and so now, here I got sixty, seventy injured troops. I'm responsible for them, there's no weapon, they're hungry, I'm hungry, I've got to keep them alive, and you can hear the clips going in the guns outside. Smoky, which is this helicopter that's shooting all the time, and the mortars are coming in, and then one night, oh Jesus, a friend of mine that I knew from Japan comes in. She's absolutely petrified. She is just scared to death and she walks up to me, she says, "I got to ask you something." I say, "What?" The nurses' quarters are being hit with rockets and she is beside herself and she says, "Tell me what this is," and she hands me the tail of a B4 rocket. I said, "Where in the hell did you get that from?" She said, "I bent over to tie my boots, and it hit my wall, over my head." There's never any rest time because as long as the battle is going, you got to go.

I'm the senior nurse because I've been in combat for a long time, and I think I'm pretty good. I mean, you got to be pretty good at this point in time, and Tet starts. We take the first round about 1:30, and this rocket comes in and it hits the hospital. They come in like ninety going west, and I mean the rockets are coming in, mortars are coming in, and I know the hospital. You can tell when the mortars and rockets hit something, and they're close. There's a lull. I'm a senior nurse and I know what's going to happen. We had those radio phones. When you say, "This is Captain Allen, over," it rings. Everybody starts screaming, because nobody wanted to get up and do that, so it was me, and a girl named Barbara. She had been with the 8th Field Hospital, and she was combat, and I'm combat. The phone rings. I know that the phone is for me. Who else can it be for? It's a chief nurse. "Captain Allen, you've got to go to work." We're about 2, 2:15 in the morning. I said to her, "Where do I have to go?" and she said, "Your unit is going to be the one open. They closed down one unit, and now we have to go on emergency run. You're going to have to go and take over because I got a second lieutenant on and I know she's petrified." So I said, "Is somebody going to walk with me, because we would have about what would be equivalent to three-quarters of a regular city block," and there's a silence. She said, "We have nobody. Wear both helmets and your flak jacket and you're on your own." I thought, whew. When I walk out, the hospital's burning. Oh Jesus, fires are everywhere, the dirt's still settling, and when I get to the unit where these kids are, these combat troops have fallen out of the beds. Jesus, their wounds are bleeding, and this second lieutenant, she's just running with her head down, because she don't know what to do. She's a baby. She don't know even that much about nursing, and she now is responsible for these kids. I think, "Oh my, I have to do something and I got to do it quick," because some of these kids are going to die just from falling out of the bed. It's these kinds of experiences, and these are constant.

The army flies medevac and that is in country. When I get there they tell me that I have to fly medevac. Golly, I wasn't there two weeks, three weeks, before it's my turn. They tell me you want to lay down to sleep and you got to be with all your clothes on. So I'm laying there, because they tell me I got to sleep light. I don't know how else you can sleep when you're under the 750s that are going off all the time. The rain comes, the chopper is five minutes out, and I have to meet it on the pad. They say put on your flak jacket and put on both helmets. They come in two helmets, right? There's a liner that you wear most of the time and then there's the big part, so I put them on and I'm standing here, it is absolutely black, I can see nothing. I can hear the chopper come in, and then it sets down. I'm supposed to run and get on and there's just a little bit of light. I get in and immediately the door closes. I said, "Well, what am I to do?" The door gunner says, "He's right there." I said, "Where?" I can hear him, he's like, "Gasp, gasp," I thought oh shit, I got a sucking chest wound, and I said, "Where's the light?" You don't fly with lights. So I've got this kid, laying here on the floor with a sucking chest wound, dying, and I got to keep this kid alive until we get to Saigon. This chopper was flying treetop high, ground ammunition is going off all around you, and then they tell me if an emergency call comes, we have to set you off and you'll have to wait until we get back. I've got to keep this kid alive. I've got to just worry about this chopper being shot out of the air, and I got to do all this in the dark. Only thing I know to do is to find his face and do breathing for this kid, and I do that all the way to Saigon. I keep him alive in the dark. We set down, they pick him up, they take him off, and we're back up again and moving. I think, those kinds of experiences can break you.

All those soldiers belonged to somebody. They got moms, they got wives, they got kids, they got somebody who loves them. I can decide to stay on. This is during the draft. They can't make that decision. They have to go. They're nineteen, they're eighteen. I did what I needed to do, I had no guilt, I have no anger. Let's face it, we have weak men and we have weak women. We have women that will break and we have men that will break. Situations can break anybody, and we have to face it, and as a country, we have men and women, and we got to deal with that, and make arrangements for that, and when we come back, there has got to be a place for women to go, where people listen.

We could recognize everybody, and because I don't run around wearing camouflage uniforms all the time, and saying I'm a Vietnam veteran, that doesn't mean that I don't have long nights. Because I do. But I have to deal with that, and as a woman veteran you often have to deal with that by yourself, because people's response to me would be, "Well, you had a choice not to go," and I always say, "But your brother didn't." I have to be able to put it in perspective, because there are a lot of women out there, who are really falling apart and who are dying. And who are dying all by themselves.

God knows I am not a martyr, trust me, but sometimes because I'm as educated as I am, because I speak well, people ask me where I stand. I don't have a lot to lose. People say, "Well, what if somebody kills you?" Death is a part of life, but if I go down, not having spoken out, then the experience is useless. We've got to look at what's going to happen to the young girls who join these combat units, and whether or not the government's going to be able to take care of them. It's a women's issue. If we don't pay attention to women in war, and America loves a war. . . . I have a university professor who says, "Well, you know I've never seen a war that I didn't like." Yeah that's because you never had to fight in one. Women deal with those kinds of traumas, and they deal with them alone. Women in war is only one more experience, even though it's more intense and more traumatic over longer periods of time. Women cannot always speak for themselves. If a woman speaks forcefully, she's seen as a bra-burner and we turn her off as one of them. If she doesn't speak at all, the issue is not taken up, and somewhere, men have got to listen so that they can speak.

The one thing that I would say that we need to know, that we don't address, is that women are warriors, the same as men are warriors, and what this country owes them, if "owe" is the word, is the same as we give any warrior. Every time we sing the "Star Spangled Banner" and we really get off on, "And the rockets red glare/The bombs bursting in the air/Gave proof through the night/That our flag was still there," remember there are soldiers, both men and women, that have given you that assurance, and you owe for that assurance. If you don't want to pay it, don't sing this summer. Does that make any sense?

Born in Huntington, West Virginia, in 1940, to John and Narcissus Allen, Elizabeth had three brothers and one sister. Her mother died of tuberculosis when Elizabeth was four. She and her siblings went to live with her grandmother, then sixty-five years of age, who raised the chil-

dren with no public assistance. Because it was the time of enforced segregation, Elizabeth attended a local two-room, all-black elementary school. After the second Supreme Court decision in 1956, she entered a previously all-white high school. Her dream was to become a civil engineer and build roads and bridges. Financing a college education was impossible, so her grandmother talked her into nursing, believing that once a registered nurse, she could pay for college herself. That never happened. Nursing became her career and her life. In 1961, she graduated from St. Mary's School of Nursing, Huntington, West Virginia. She entered Ohio State University in 1963. Two years later she received a Baccalaureate in nursing science. That year, when Elizabeth was twenty-three, her father died of complications from chronic alcoholism. In 1966 she received her Master's degree in psychiatric nursing. She then joined the army and went to Vietnam. After leaving the military in 1969 she worked for South Carolina as State Director of Psychiatric Nursing. After two years she left that position to attend the University of South Carolina. In 1973 she received a Ph.D. in elementary guidance from the University of South Carolina. She has the distinction of being the first African American woman to earn a Ph.D. from that university. Over the years Allen worked as an appointee to the commission studying the effects of Agent Orange. With her special concern being African Americans, she has been a consultant to the Veteran's Administration regarding treatment of veterans for PTSD, cancer, and homelessness. Congressman Charles Rangell (D – NY) appointed Allen to the Black Veteran Braintrust in an advisory capacity to the Congressional Black Caucus on the status of African American veterans. She has one son with Attention Deficit Disorder who completed college and teaches in Detroit. Elizabeth Allen continues to work for the rights of women veterans. Presently she is an associate professor at the University of Michigan School of Nursing, Ann Arbor.

Joan Garvert
Army Nurse

After her first assignment in Fort Lee, Virginia, as an army nurse, freshly minted 2nd Lieutenant Joan Garvert was on her way to Vietnam with only three weeks' notice in February 1970. Her first stop, as with many nurses, was the sprawling base of Long Binh near Saigon. Soon, though, she was in Phu Bai, northern I Corps at the 85th Evacuation Hospital, recently moved from Qui Nhon. It was a small hospital and she worked on the surgical ward taking care of men after surgery, after they had been in intensive care, and when they were recovering from their wounds.

I'm one of six children, and my dad had said every one of us was going to have a college education and I saw the army as a way to help my dad out to get us all through. Get myself through college any way. They had the student nurse program, and if you gave them one year, then you owed them two, if you gave them two years, I think, you owed them three. The re-

101

cruiter came around to our college, just recruiting, and they of course, like everybody else, promised that you will not go to Vietnam unless you request to go. So I didn't sign up until my last year of college.

When we got to basic training, the word out of every instructor's mouth was, "When you get to Vietnam you will find it this way," and we kept saying, "You know, we aren't signed up to go to Vietnam," and they continued saying, "When you get to Vietnam, this is the way things will be," not *if* you go.

I remember it well, hearing about going. I was stationed at Fort Lee, Virginia, and I had just come in from grocery shopping at the PX, about $30 worth of groceries, which in those days was the entire month's worth of groceries. I received a phone call and I had to drop everything to answer the phone. The chief nurse or colonel at our hospital got on the phone and she said, "You've been relieved of duty here at Fort Lee, Virginia." All I could think was, "What have I done now, what have I screwed up, you know, what have I done?" Then she said, "Your orders for Vietnam are here," and down went the phone. She didn't give me a chance to say one thing. I immediately called over to the hospital to where my girlfriend was working. The head nurse over there heard my voice and got my girlfriend to the phone but she immediately said another one just got her orders. So, it was sort of like a pattern they did.

I was excited, frankly. You know, I mean, this was going to be a new adventure. Scared of course. I don't remember my folks' response. I know I had to have called and told them. I think they were just mute, not knowing what to say.

I was leaving for Fort Dix and I had already left my home and arrived in Virginia a little bit early. Then I stopped in to where I had been just stationed and they told me that I had just totally overpacked and everything, and you can't take this, and you can't take that. I met a nurse who had been there already and she says, "You're a woman, you can take anything you want because they're going to let you carry anything on board you want. You're special because you're a woman," and that kind of thing. She definitely made me feel better. The other nurse had me worried. She thought I should throw everything out of my duffel bag that was stupid to take.

There were a bunch of us women on the plane. I'd say maybe close to a dozen. I don't know if that's unusual or not. I can remember everybody with their sort of anticipating attitudes and I got a kick out of some of the women that were dressed so fancy. They were in their high heels, they had their hair all up on their heads and all. The plane ride is about twenty-four hours. I thought, "Here we are on this plane to Vietnam. We don't know what our future holds for us," and I really just was distressed at this particular flight. The airline stewardesses just had no humor whatsoever. They served us only milk or water, something like that. They would not even serve you sodas, or anything that could be mixed with booze, if you had snuck any booze on board—I thought to lighten up the women, you know. We stopped in Hawaii for layover, just a couple of hours on the ground and then Guam. By the time we got there it was a different scene.

Everybody had their short skirts and bouffant hairdos. That's the main thing I can think of. We had our uniform skirts that we'd roll the waistbands to get them a little shorter, and things like that. Once we were out of where we were supposed to be, you were not supposed to have earrings on like everybody else had—you were to look very professional.

We landed at Tan Son Nhut and we were taken to Long Binh. Instant humidity hitting you and you're thinking, "Well, my hair for a year will not ever look the same again," and everything. I guess because it was the airport it was not only the humidity, but the odors from the planes and everything just really socked you in the face. When we got there, there was no one there actually to meet us for a long, long time. None of us knew where we were to go. It was just sort of that we felt like lost souls frankly. No one really wanted to be messed with us, as far as to get us where we needed to go.

They finally came and picked us up on a bus that had the wires on the windows and everything, and told us not to joke with anybody because the guys with the guns had been there twenty-four hours more than we had and they were scared out of their wits and could easily shoot anybody because they were so scared. And then, I don't know what you call it any more, they took us to—it wasn't barracks—where they were going to relocate you to decide where we would be sent. We met with the chief nurse of Vietnam and she asked us where we wanted to be stationed, if anybody had any preferences. I didn't know a thing about Vietnam, and so she just told me that I would go to the 85th evac hospital. I said, "Well I have a friend that's coming three weeks later, any chance we could be together?" "No, no, you can't be together," she said. She ended up joining me three weeks later.

Definitely by the 1970s it was winding down and from what I heard people talking, it was definitely a different flavor of war. The Vietnamese people's attitudes were totally different. Instead of seeing you as someone that's come to help, you were seen more as the enemy. You know, you were the ones that were corrupt, is the way I felt like they saw us. By that time, enough corruption had gone on that the GIs, or Americans I should say, had brought corruption into their country. I mean, as far as the Vietnamese women, when they would see us they were sort of in awe of the American women, they would always come up and point at us. We were always so much taller built, our hair was certainly a different color than theirs.

After Saigon they flew us by C-130 up to Danang. In Danang we then got on a helicopter. My actual way of getting into action was a little different than most people's because they put us on these two helicopters that were headed up north that were used for medevacs. Probably because of all of us being on the plane, plus our luggage, the helicopter I was on blew a compressor, and it started going down. It went into auto rotation and it would have landed safely if it hadn't been for the excess luggage and people on board. So we dropped about one hundred feet out of the sky. The pilot could have landed. We were over water. He got us onto the beach, and the helicopter actually was sort of partially buried. I'm going to call them runners, and I think the tail boom broke off on it. We were following another helicopter and it saw what happened to us and came back and picked us up.

Well, it was a bit of a wake-up call because we were sitting on a stretcher. I and two other women, and I was right smack in the middle of the stretcher, and when we landed, the stretcher broke in three different places where each of us were sitting because of the impact. Because of our luggage I had my feet under me under the stretcher, and until everybody else got up, I couldn't get my legs out, and I was probably the last one to leave the ship. I attempted to stand up. When I did, that helicopter was now about three feet shorter than it had been because it was buried in the sand. One of the crewmen knocked me to the ground which, thank goodness he did, because the blade was still going around and would have gotten my head. Then he started trying to pull me. Because my legs had been pinned, they had been sort of like rubber and wouldn't work very well. He's pulling me with one hand and I really only had this one hand I was working with and finally I just yelled at them and didn't say anything real nice at the moment to him, trying to get his attention to please let me go so I could at least use two hands. And we crawled away from the helicopter, and the other helicopter came back, picked us up. We were medevaced to the hospital where we were going to work. When we came in, they admitted us to make sure we were all okay. The helicopter crew came to check on us and see how we were doing. I said, "Would you say hi to," and I can't remember his name, I wish I could. They said, "He's scared of you." I said, "Why in the world is he scared of me?" He says, "Well, you yelled at him and you're an officer." And I thought, "Lordy, you know, I just wanted to be able to stop eating sand while being dragged, and to get away, anyway." He was just a real sweetheart. The first three days I was a patient. When I finally got my uniform back, I realized that the back of my uniform was totally saturated in fuel oil and that if there had been a fire I would have been burned. So that was the biggest eye-opener I think of all . . . seeing my uniform when I got it back.

Then they put us in a hooch, you know, where we were assigned and my luggage caught up with me. You were assigned a ward and I was assigned to the surgical ward. There were two wards at the 85th at that time in Phu Bai. Phu Bai is south of Hue and north of Danang. It's right smack on the main highway that went north and south in Vietnam. There was a big air base right behind us. Camp Eagle was nearby. That was where we did our shopping, if you got to go. I mean, it wasn't walking distance whatsoever. Usually someone had to take you. There was also an intensive care unit, and surgical wards, the one ward we kept everybody that was a little bit more serious. It had IV fluids, it required a little bit more care and we worked on both of those wards, we'd relieve each other on those wards.

We did not come under attack when I was there. I have to say I was very, very lucky. There would be a couple of times when we were told that there had been snipers seen in the area, and we were under alert, but never at the time I was there, like some of the other nurses have described.

They were twelve-hour days. Your days started at seven and you had the little nurses' area, your hooch, that was separate from the men. They had a fence around us women. You tried to get in there while there was still hot water, to get cleaned up in the morning. Got to work at seven, and immediately for me, I started preparing all the IV medications for the entire day for a twenty-four-hour period. In those days, we didn't have all the fancy equipment. We had to do everything by hand, so drawing up and mixing every one of these IVs was the beginning of my day while someone else went around and checked the patients. Usually the corpsmen helped the patients with any of their care, and did most of the dressings, frankly.

We had doctors but they were always in surgery all day, and would just come over afterwards to check. We were an evacuation hospital, so that meant that every day you got the patients that were about to be shipped out, which was usually about half the patients. Then the new batch would come in that afternoon. They would stay one full day and, if ready, they would be shipped out the next day. So our patients were never there but say one full day, two half days, and you had to get them all ready to be ready to go.

I saw the men by the time that they had already come through the emergency room, and had been to surgery. This was for their aftercare. To make sure that they were stable and everything was ready for transport. We had a large percentage of cellulitis which is just an inflammation of tissue that's become infected and very prevalent over there. We had people come in from bumping into their foot locker where they got a bruise on their leg, a hematoma. It would turn into a site of infection and end up having to be opened and drained. Stateside, that never would have happened. A mosquito bite or something. I had one guy came in with his entire shoulder where it was so large you just thought it was going to pop, and that was just from a mosquito bite. See, that's the cellulitis part of it, and there was a great deal of that. We had some amputations, a lot of shrapnel wounds. We'd get in some Vietnamese that were postpartum, I took care of a brand new baby one night. We used to get on our one ward a lot of children that we would put over there that the doctors were doing some reconstructive work on, or some of them with burns or things like that. We had, in particular, a couple of patients I remember, that had burns on the entire back...where their back had been exposed.

We were treating Vietnamese, yeah. Some of the hospitals had wards that were strictly Vietnamese. We were a small hospital, and the main Vietnamese we had were, what they had, say the children that the doctors had taken a particular interest in helping. Adult-wise, there were a few. We had the Kit Carson scouts, which at the time was a new term to me. These were, I think, North Vietnamese that were helping the Americans, and they were very valuable soldiers to have.

It amazed me I was never one that, before Vietnam, ever went camping with my family. I did not like it at all. I was amazed at how well I adapted over there. Even though you were away from your family, the people you worked with were your family suddenly. You missed knowing what was going on at home. I really felt very cut off from that, but they did become my family over there.

I remember we were having such an influx of wounded that they even took our movie house and made it another ward. They put beds up in it, which gave me three wards to be checking when I worked night shift. We just had so many that we couldn't accommodate everybody. I was handling dozens of patients. I want to say each of the two main wards had maybe thirty apiece on them and they put up an extra ten beds. You know, as I say in my thirty-year recollection of it, they didn't keep that open very long. As soon as they could get people to move out they did. The guys were always very, very nice to us. The corpsmen were great, the patients just, you know, they were so happy to see us, to feel safe, to have a real bed to sleep in, to have, as they said, a round eye to talk to. I mean, it was never, hardly anything more than where are you from, you know, things like that. Just small time passing, but still, I can't ever remember anybody being disrespectful or anything.

The most critical weren't over on our ward. I remember one guy in particular, he stayed with us more than the usual time. Because of his injuries he couldn't be transported. In the middle of the night we had the operator call and say they could put through a M.A.R.S.[2] call, and did anyone want to make a call? And he said yeah, he would. Well, because he couldn't get out of bed, we ended up moving his bed up to the front desk. I had just given him a pain shot because he had so many wounds and we had just got through dressing everything, and he was a little high on his Demerol. I'm listening to him talk to his mother on the phone, "No, I'm just fine, everything's going fine here." She had no idea that he was in the hospital. He said he wouldn't bother telling her that until later. But there were some that were very concerned how their wives were going to receive them, according to what injury they had.

[2.] A military telephone system.

They weren't there long enough to counsel. Our guys were moved out so fast. I was a very short-term counselor, if I was, but you didn't have time and at that point they weren't there long enough out from the field to have those concerns yet. This was early stage. This was when they were just thankful that they were alive, and their injuries weren't worse than they were.

I felt so ill prepared to be there.

I was, "lucky" is exactly the term to use. Those that worked in the intensive care unit, the extent of injuries that they saw was so horrendous. When they did come back and they'd have a chance to talk, they'd be telling me what they were seeing over in the intensive care unit. I went over there a couple of times because I just couldn't imagine what they were talking about, and to have worked with that every day, I think would have been extremely difficult. I'm glad I was on the ward where I was. Nurses didn't cry. We just didn't. You had all of yourself together. You couldn't allow that.

My entire year I considered, for years and years, the best year of my life . . . the best year of my life. I felt like I was needed, that I was doing something useful, that what I was doing I knew how to do and I knew how to do it well and that I walked away and had satisfaction from. When I came home, I didn't have that satisfaction anymore in my nursing for many years.

It was a special feeling that you kept inside you. You came home feeling oh like, you knew so much, had experienced so much more of life than the people around you. I can remember my mom wanting me to get together with my old classmates from school. I had a hard time sitting there with them, listening to them, those that were married talking about their babies, the other ones whether so-and-so was going to call them. I just wanted to scream out, don't you realize there's people dying on the other side of the world, aren't you concerned about that? I didn't open my mouth, but it was just very frustrating. My friends were all into their own little world. They wanted to talk about their babies, their lives now, who they were dating, whether so-and-so would call them, and I just couldn't deal with it because there were people dying on the other side of the world. I thought, don't you all understand what's going on in the world? I was out drinking one night with my friends in a bar and when I walked in the bar the juke box was playing, and then all of a sudden the live band came back on and the drummer did a drum roll. Well, the drum roll just about put me way under the bar. It just so totally unnerved me for the rest of the evening. Well, you just had a feeling that you were being attacked, that roll you know. . . . That was incoming.

Right before I left Vietnam they were beginning to move troops into Laos. Every day for a good week or two before I left you could look at the air field sitting right next to the hospital and the helicopters were coming in for refueling. There were so many of them in the sky it looked like mosquitoes, and you knew they were heading further north, that there was going to be so much action. I was sitting right next to Highway 1, the tanks were bumper to bumper on that road, all moving north, and you just knew that there was something terrible going to happen. They were going to need your help, and that's why I didn't want to come home. I mean, I just felt terrible, like you were deserting your men. You were already there and you were already trained and that would be useful to them, and you hated to leave.

I knew that my parents were under a great deal of stress with me being over there, that I needed to get back home. I could have extended. I guess I could have extended quite a bit, maybe if I wanted. I definitely could have extended thirty days and then get an early out from the service, but I chose not to do that.

When I was working in the hospital and would hear a helicopter bringing a patient to the helipad I was glued to that window. I just had to see it, I had to know what was happening. When we were over there, we didn't have windows, but you heard them coming in and as soon as your helicopters were coming in, you could tell by the speed that they came in how serious the patient was. I mean, I wasn't in the emergency room triage area or anything, but you heard the helicopters. Number one, you knew if you heard them as close as we did, that they were coming to us, and say the speed at which they came in, you knew whether it was someone critical, or how many helicopters came in, how much influx of patients you were going to have. Then for a long time I couldn't figure out why, but certain odors very much reminded me of Vietnam. Some things I couldn't even figure out why. One of the simple things was Dial soap. I thought why is Dial soap bothering me? Then I realized that was the brand of soap that we had over there, and every time I thought I smelled Dial soap I thought of my year. Stupid, but that's what happens—just little things.

Yeah, my feelings have changed. The fact that you realize that they really didn't want us there anymore. Some of it you can understand, why they didn't want us there, because of, say, black market, and the young girls with their prostitution was tearing their families apart. The war was totally changing things. And the GIs—I think by the time I got there, drugs had become very prevalent and they hadn't been early in the war. I didn't like seeing what it was doing to them. We were overdue to get out, I thought. You know, we weren't accomplishing anything anymore.

The reports were changed, figures were changed over there as to what was really happening. I think it still goes on today, either who's killed or injured or how it happened or anything like that. Trust was a big thing that's changed. I still don't trust our government. I take everything with a grain of salt. Greater appreciation for little things in life. I'm very thankful for the friends I have. They mean a great deal to me.

We were definitely there so that they could continue doing what they were supposed to. I mean, we were patching them up. We definitely had our role there too. And it was an important role. It wasn't just the nurses. There were so many other women there too, the Red Cross, Special Services, the civilians, and some other of these people I didn't even know existed while I was there except for the one Red Cross girl that was stationed with our hospital. Otherwise, I really was not aware of the extent of the women over there, just like most men are not, and some men will still say today, "I never saw an American woman over there. . . . There weren't any."

Well, I don't think today people who have attended enough events would say it, but I can remember when we were trying to get our memorial, signing petitions to get our Vietnam Women's Memorial, you'd ask veterans, and they would say, "No, I will not sign it, there were no women in Vietnam." And I remember one reply. I used to say, "Well, I'm glad you never saw a woman in Vietnam because that means that you were never injured," or something, because that's when primarily they did see the nurses.

I would go again if I was that age again. Yeah, yeah I would. I wish at this age, I felt like I would be able to. It was a worthwhile experience.

Joan Garvert was born and brought up in Springfield, Illinois, the second oldest of four sisters and one brother. Her father was a veterinarian, and her mother taught school for two years before becoming a full-time homemaker devoted to taking care of their growing family. Garvert attended an all-girls Catholic high school, and entered Quincy College with the thought of becoming a teacher. After one year that paled, and Joan decided to become a nurse. She says, "Teaching and nursing were

about the only two professions then open to young women and I chose nursing." After transferring to Southern Illinois State University at Edwardsville, she graduated in the spring of 1969 and went to South Vietnam in early 1970. She returned as a 1st Lieutenant from Vietnam in February 1971. At loose ends, she says she was a nervous wreck and wanted to stay in a cocoon, at least for a while. She lived at home for a year and then moved to Fort Lee, Virginia, where she worked in a civilian hospital. Joan soon quit because she found the hospital and its ideas for nursing "backward and old-fashioned" compared to what she had done and seen in Vietnam. She then went to work for the federal government. She has worked for the Veteran's Administration in Atlanta, St. Louis, Biloxi, Tampa, Decatur, Illinois, and Springfield, Illinois. Garvert earned her Master's degree in surgical nursing from Southern Illinois University. She stays in nursing, she says, "Because I care and I want to do a decent job."

KATHLEEN SPLINTER
ARMY NURSE

Kathleen Splinter joined the WACs, the Women's Army Corps, in her junior year, to help pay for nursing school. After graduating in 1966 Kathy arrived in Vietnam not as a WAC but as an army nurse. Her assignment was at the 312th Evacuation Hospital in Chu Lai, northern I Corps. Only 70 miles from the DMZ, Chu Lai was home to the U.S. Army's 23rd Division, better known as the American Division, famous for fighting in the Pacific in World War II. Chu Lai, the southern anchor of I Corps, was an area of some of the war's most intense fighting.

I enrolled in the Army Nurse Corps Program to pay for my last year in school. I enrolled when I was a junior, and I was actually in the Women's Army Corps until I passed my boards a year after I graduated from nursing school, and then I was commissioned. I had two years to serve for that year of financial help.

Originally I was stationed at Fort Bragg, North Carolina. I had already made plans to be married. I had met somebody at Fort Bragg, and had been told that I would not be going to Vietnam. The process of getting married in the army is that you have to seek request, or approval, from your higher ups. We made all the arrangements to get married and then about two weeks before I was married, the orders were canceled. I was told I wasn't going to be going to Vietnam. So I was just ecstatic that I wasn't going to have to go Vietnam. I was married on Labor Day, and the week after I got back from my honeymoon there were orders waiting for me to go. So a month and four days later I went to Vietnam. I just thought it was the way the army did things.

I was only at Fort Bragg from January until September, October when I left, and it was very, very busy. Fort Bragg had a huge, basic training and AIT program and I was in the medical unit. During the winter months these kids would just get sick and the ward that usually had, say, thirty patients went to six or seven hundred people because these guys, if they had a temperature over a certain amount, they had to be admitted to the hospital for observation because they didn't want to have problems with them. So I mean we were working ten-hour shifts at Fort Bragg. I was highly indignant about it because I didn't have a choice in it. We were just busy where I was working. I wasn't aware of what was going on.

We didn't know at first we were going to Vietnam because they were secret orders. They were secret orders, yeah, and there was a whole list and it was people that I knew that I had gone through basic with and everything, but no destination. I mean, however you read that mumbo jumbo that orders come down in. But no, we were part of a nursing and medical complement for a hospital unit and we were all leaving from Fort

Lewis, Washington, so I assumed that we were all going to Vietnam, but until we touched down we didn't know concretely. Everybody else in the plane was going to Vietnam, but our orders didn't tell us, which I also thought was a little strange.

There were forty-some nurses and twelve or fifteen doctors, and we were all assigned to this hospital, but we didn't know where it was going to be. It just is amazing. I know they did those kinds of things, supposedly in World War II. At least I've seen them in movies, but it's hard to live it. The plane held three hundred-and-some people and maybe sixty of us didn't know where we were going and everybody else was going to Vietnam. We walked off the plane about fifteen past midnight. I will never forget it. I swear the army leaves and takes off and touches down in dark, and when you walked out of the plane you hit this wall of humidity. It was incredible, and the smell was—it had to have been in the tropics. This was the first time I'd ever seen it or smelled it, but it was like walking in a wall of humidity. Hot, oh, unbelievable, hot, hot, hot. It was awful.

I sat with two girls that were actually from Fort Bragg. One girl I had lived with for a short period of time. There were a bunch of nurses that lived together, and I had known Barbara. She was about ten years older than me, a very elegant lady and she's a friend even to this day. She became a mentor and we were talking about things we wouldn't do because we were ladies. We weren't going to take any kind of community showers, we thought that was a little indignant and they couldn't force us to do that. It was a twenty-some-odd hour trip to Vietnam and we touched down in a couple of places and the only thing that they consistently gave us was either beans or corn on the flight, so it was a real unusual flight going over. When we touched down we were all dressed in summer cords with nylons and pumps and the little handbag and everything else.

We walk into this heat, they didn't know what to do with us. They didn't have any bathroom facilities for us, and we stood around, literally stood around in this dirty building and guys were sleeping on the floor and sleeping on the few benches that they had and they would sort of open their eyes and look at us and turn away. Coming from America I had never been treated that way, just sort of dismissed, you know, and I thought, "Oh, how rude." Somebody tried to call somebody in to try to make arrangements for us. Around six o'clock in the morning we were all put on a bus and taken to some air force facility to eat. Then we were taken on a plane, a C-130, to go to Tan San Nhut to the 90th Replacement Hospital where we were going to find out all our orders. I mean, by that time we had been up over twenty-four hours, probably closer to thirty-six or forty hours, and you're sort of in a fog, and you're scared to death, but it was a big adventure because we were all together by that time. It was all sixty of us. There was no water to drink, and it was just—I think at that point it was just still an adventure to us.

I will never forget it as long as I live. It was outhouses they had. They had to clear out this BOQ [Bachelor Officers' Quarters] because there was so many of us and usually the women would only go in one or two at a time, and they were put up in air-conditioned trailers. Well, there was too many of us. So they cleared out this BOQ and we were assigned to bunks. I was in the top bunk because the girl that was in the bottom bunk, I think a nutritionist or something, she was leaving at four in the morning so she wanted to get out of bed without disturbing me. Rita and Barbara, who are the two girls I sat with going over, were in the next cubicle and we got to bed. It was just an insult. By that time I didn't care if the whole Vietnamese Army watched me take a shower, you just wanted to be clean, you were so dirty, and the sprockets didn't work. It was just a three-ring circus. We had all fallen asleep, and all of a sudden the alarm goes off, the sirens were wailing, things were falling on the roof. We didn't know what was happening. I almost decapitated the poor girl on the bottom bunk just jumping out of the bed. Almost killed myself, but if I was going to die I wanted to die with Barbara and Rita, at least I knew them. We were trying to find our flashlights and get together. We think what happened was the BOQ was right next to Highway 1, which we were told was unsafe. It was all barbed wire and everything, and we think that he was just shooting from a watchtower, or threw rocks on us. It was metal roofs, corrugated roofs and caused a scene, just to see these nurses running around in the middle of the night. That was my first night, within twenty-four hours of arriving. Scared the living daylights out of us. Then you woke up the next morning and you were uncomfortable. It was hot, you were scared to death, and you think this isn't quite what I thought, but we were there.

I just remember watching all the stories on TV, and I thought we'd be safe. We were told over and over again, at least I was, by family members, by people who knew that I was going to the service, "Oh, don't worry because nurses are in safe positions." So I think that I didn't explore any further. I didn't know where to go with that, and I just trusted that they were telling me the truth, that no nurse had been killed since World War II. I thought, "Okay, I can get used to noise." We weren't safe, and we hadn't been prepared to take care of ourselves if anything happened. I think of all the things, that's one of the things that really bothers me to this day, that we were placed in harm's way. Several hospitals were overrun and the nurses were really a burden then, at that point. Had anything happened, they couldn't participate in safely defending themselves, or defending anybody else. You put a gun in my hand and I'm a danger because we weren't considered smart enough to handle it. When I was in basic, the captain that taught us our weapons—we only learned with a .45—but he told us, "Just sight, because if you ever have to defend yourself, you won't know how to use the gun," and they wouldn't give us live ammunition. I'd never fired a gun and I just thought, "Well, that's sort of strange." But then, we are going to be safe, so I guess we don't need it, and I think sometimes we probably did need it.

For a long time I just wanted to leave. We were so busy. When we finally got to Chu Lai, it was a big adventure getting there. The monsoons were just starting and we were delayed five days because of it. We went to Danang and we couldn't get out from Danang to go to Chu Lai and we thought, "Well, this is interesting, what's happening?" Even then when you walked around the hospital area, the 95th at Danang, and you said "Hello" to people which I had always been taught, especially as a nurse, you greeted people, you greeted patients, you greeted staff, people just sort of looked at you, and again, there was this dismissal. I can remember talking and saying I'm not going to become like that. I don't know what's wrong with these girls because it was nurses that were doing this, and it was only because of Sharon Lane later, eight or nine months later, that I realized that I had changed and was doing the same thing. It was such an insidious change day by day, that you started protecting yourself a little bit more, and plus you didn't have a lot of outlets, going to see other people, you know. You were really in your little confines of wherever you were assigned.

You got into your mode, you could do your nursing work, and it was safe there, but when somebody else, somebody new came in and then demanded something new, or—and this is all a perception on your part—if you thought they were giving you that feedback that you had changed, that was very challenging to you. That was very frightening, at least to me it was. You know when new people would come in and they'd be so bouncy and energetic and fresh, and enthusiastic and alive, I think it was then at those moments that I realized that I had changed. Yet, what do you do with it, you still had to go and work your twelve hours, you still had to go and do the things that, quote, "nurses" were supposed to do, but certainly I had not been prepared for.

We worked twelve-hour shifts, it was seven to seven, night or day, and you worked six days a week. I was married at the time so I worked a lot of nights because, what were you going to do at night? Some of the single girls dated or you'd go to the officer's club or something, I didn't choose to do that, I didn't choose to make myself that lonely. I loved dancing and every-thing else and why place yourself in harm's way or tempta-tion's way? That was my thinking, so I'd work a lot of nights. You go on, you'd do rounds, get your assignment and I got into the intensive care unit. There was a nineteen bed intensive care unit. I had never worked an intensive care unit in my life. In fact, the hospital that I graduated from did not have an in-tensive care unit except for the last six months of my training and so it was sick people that were literally blown apart, Viet-namese prisoners as well as GIs. My first day in the intensive care unit was hard. There were like six or seven tracheotomies. I had seen one in my three years of school, and never a fresh one. It was the corpsman, I will never forget him teaching me how to do it. You'd go in as a young nurse thinking you have all of this experience and it was humbling in a lot of ways to real-ize that you really were barely scratching the surface, and then you just started to help one another. You know, I hope that I was able to help some of the corpsmen do their work because they certainly helped me learn about what I had to do. I don't know how they did it, but they really rose to the occasion.

You just took care of what was there. Sometimes we'd have to evacuate people because there would be "rushers" coming in, and it took me a long, long time after I got home to put together facts or information because we were working so hard in those nineteen beds with such a short staff. What went on outside, I don't know, you know, I mean unless you went to the blood bank, or you ran to get some kind of supplies, you were there your twelve hours, and a lot, many times longer than that, so, I mean it was a very full day.

I was just one of the team. Barbara was our head nurse. She was a captain, I was a second lieutenant when I first went over. I became a first lieutenant, which was an automatic thing. The rank didn't mean very much to me. There were like six or seven girls that we worked with and we all graduated the same year. We all had a year under our belts, and there were a couple of male nurses that I worked with that graduated within a year or two of me. We were all brand new kids on the block, doing our best, flying by the seat of our pants, and just praying that we weren't hurting too many people because God, it didn't take a rocket scientist to know that we were in over our heads. We just kept literally trying to do the best that we could and learn from our mistakes and go on and not make the same ones again. I mean, it's incredible what the human body can take, both for the patient and those taking care of them, because it was overwhelming, it was overwhelming.

We used our senses more than I ever did stateside. I learned that by looking you could tell somebody was going sour without having all of the equipment around. We didn't have any kind of monitors, we didn't have any special equipment, we had our eyes and ears, and that was about it. We had blood pressure cups, we had antiquated suction machines, and that was it. The only time we ever used one monitor was when somebody was expected to die. We weren't going to be able to do anything for them. They were behind curtains and you'd hook them up so that when it was a straight line you could call Graves Registration because you were too busy to spend time. It always bothered me that we did that. I felt there was some part of me that was saying this is wrong, somebody should be with this person. They were young kids that were dying, but we were too busy. We found out years after I came home, that we got a citation at the 312th. That the hospital got a citation for being one of the busiest hospitals in Vietnam for our ten months in country. We were just so busy, I can't remember from December until July. I can't tell you months. I know that I was there, I know when I went on vacation in May, I know when Sharon died and I know when I left, and those were my points of reference, but I couldn't tell you anything about anything else.

There are some patients that stand out. There was one, he was a Puerto Rican young man and he called himself Tom and he was blown apart. He had all kinds of injuries, and for some reason he could remember my name and he was with us a long time. Usually the patients that went through us were evaced out as soon as they were stable, but we kept our patients with us for a long period of time if they were just too sick to be evacuated out.

He was one of those who went to surgery several times. He was really sick, fractures, head wounds, belly wounds, chest wounds, the whole thing. He was bilingual so when he would call out sometimes it was broken English, but he could remember my name and he would always ask for a bed pan. I

can remember him saying so many times, "Cotty, I need the
bed pan, I got to take a sheet," and he would scream it out
and half the time he was unconscious, and he would scream
it out. More than once he'd say, "Cotty, I need the big one,"
because there's a special bed pan that's much smaller, and
we'd always tease him about it. He used to be right next to the
nurses' stations and we'd switched him across the way to this
great big long line of beds. He was over here, because he was
doing a little, little bit better, and it was so, so busy, and I
looked up one day, and he was dead, and I was so furious that
he had died. I wanted to say I felt like I had done something
wrong, and I knew I hadn't, but we worked so hard. I remember him and I don't remember so many others. We worked so
hard with him, and he just died with no one by his bedside.
That always bothered me, that always, always bothered me,
and then it took another hour to do just the paperwork. When
it was years later, I wrote down some facts on him, that he received how many units of blood and plasma, and at the time
we were just doing it over and over and over again. Now I
know that he probably couldn't have lived just because of
everything that had happened, and yet as a young nurse I
didn't know that. I thought that he was going to make it. We
had poured our hearts into him, and he didn't make it, and
every time that happened, you just turned off a little bit more.
You just didn't get involved, but he was pretty close. That had
to have been some time in May or June, the end of May first
part of June, because he is on the Wall pretty close to Sharon
Lane, and it's chronological on the Wall. That's all I can remember about him.

   There's a couple of other patients that I can remember.
One guy was dying and he had reminded me he was from
Texas with a soft drawl. My husband spent, or my husband at

the time spent, a lot of time in Texas and he reminded me of him, that soft drawl and he turned, and was going down hill and had a trach done, and he came off the ventilator one time and plugged up his hole and started saying, "Thank you" to all of us. I kept saying, "Yeah, yeah, yeah," you know, "lay back, don't stress yourself," and he laid back and he died, and I will never get over the fact of him thanking us. I can still see him in my mind's eye, plugging up his hole and saying thank you to all of us and it wasn't until he died that I realized what he was doing, and wanting to scream. And yet you couldn't, you were on duty, you had X number of hours left to go, and then, you know, what do you do with those feelings? It just bothered you.

I think [the fact] that we remained even-keeled for the year that we were there is remarkable. I'm still in touch with a number of the girls that I served with, and I think we're in various stages of even keel-ness. I think that it was such an assault and an affront, it certainly affected me and I still live out the consequences of it. I don't know how I would have done it differently. It is such violence. Man's inhumanity to man is so awful, it's so awful, that it still takes my breath away. To see it displayed in today's society over and over and over again, even with our children now, with the school violence, when do we learn our lesson that that's not a way to go? How do we teach our children, how do we teach ourselves?

I don't think I expected either to take care of the Vietnamese civilians. We would have the whole range in intensive care. We literally had women that were also injured delivering babies. We would take care of the mother, the child, babies. Then you'd have mama-san or papa-san in the ward, because the Vietnamese families would travel with their soldiers and when the soldiers were injured, the family would come into the hospital. It was a three ring circus. They'd sometimes try to sleep underneath the bed, or they'd be parked outside, literally sleeping on the ground, wherever they could, and that was new to me. If one drop of the IV was good, they thought two drops was better and ten drops was really going to get him good. You had to watch some of the people that would adjust the IVs. You had to be aware that that could happen. They were also scroungers. I don't remember any of them stealing anything first time around, but they would take IV tubing out of the trash. They would take our trash and they would save everything. I have no idea what for, but they had nothing, absolutely nothing. That was a real stretch for me, taking care of little babies, and old people, and the young GIs, and then taking care of prisoners. It was really difficult doing that. I had no idea that we would be doing that when I went overseas.

Sharon came in, if I'm not mistaken, in mid- or late April of '69, and in fact, one of the girls that is still a very, very good friend of mine—best friend that I have in the world—came in country together. The two of them were assigned to the 312th, and Sharon lived in the BOQ across the compound from me. I remember her going on duty. On my one day off I'd be sitting outside my room. We were on the South China Sea. It was breathtakingly beautiful, and I could see her going to the end of the ramp and just looking out, and she's brand new. That was the first time we had gotten any new nurses from October to April. All of us girls that were there, all of us nurses that were there, were really tight with one another and here are these two strangers. This is when I knew I had changed, just like those girls I first saw in Danang. Now I knew I was just like them, and I hated Sharon, because she would say hello and I wouldn't respond ... me, who would say hello to everybody. I knew I was doing it, and I was angry that she said "hi" to me.

I wanted to say, "Why are you making me feel this bad about not responding to you?" It was just these flashes inside that I knew I didn't used to be like that. I didn't like myself like this. I'm ashamed to say no, I wouldn't speak to her. When she died, I was furious that she died, because she didn't hurt enough to die, because death was really a release of the pain. I think death was much more merciful than having to continue on. I still think that way. I still think that at times death isn't as awful as we think it's going to be, and I was angry at her for a long time. I was ashamed of it. I never talked about it with anybody until I started in counseling, and it took me years, a long time to get over that, to come to a sort of peace. But she was so fresh and exuberant, and one of the quotes that was attributed to her after her death was her admiration of the Vietnamese people. I can remember saying when I heard that, that because she hadn't been here long enough, she hadn't learned to hate. And I can remember saying that, and writing home and saying that, and being ashamed because I hated that much now. I knew that, and yet we put on these happy little faces as though we didn't feel that way. So it was really all turbulent.

We were hit several times. It was weird. It was not like what you would think it would even sound like. I can remember asking one of the girls that I got to know, I cannot remember her name, I said, "How will you know if it's incoming?" which was a new term to me. She said, "Don't worry, you'll know." If you remember the flicks you saw about World War II there were always alarms going off, and I wanted to know where the alarm was and who rang it, how did he know. The physical hospital used to be the 2nd Surgical Hospital. They moved up to the DMZ, and the 312th moved into their physical location. There were a couple of holdovers from the 2nd Surg that were orienting everybody and then they were going to be going home.

The 2nd Surg had taken the alarm with them, so for a couple of months we didn't have one, and I thought, "Well, that's not very fair. How are we going to know?" I was very serious. I was a little scared, and she says, "Don't worry, you'll know." It was usually mortar attacks, and I'm not even sure what a mortar looks like. I don't think I've ever seen one, but it sounded like they would set off a progression of them. It sounded like the Jolly Green Giant walking in, like you would think a heavy giant lumping ahead. Then you knew you were under attack. It was only when it was over that the alarm, when we finally got an alarm, would go off, and you think, "Well, that was effective." We were hit a couple of times but not bad, sort of right on the outskirts, and some of the doctors at one point were trying to either refurbish or build a boat. It was what they did in their spare time to use up some of their energy and skills and everything, and the boat took a direct hit. They were really upset about that. I slept through that alert and again, when you work twelve hours a day, or more, you're really tired when you get home, and when you fall asleep, you fall into a dead sleep. So I slept through a couple of them. We were hit a couple of times in the compound, but it wasn't as bad as what I had seen on TV, or what I saw lived out in the patients that I took care of, until the day Sharon was killed. That was a direct hit on the hospital. It hit the Vietnamese ward, a direct hit, and that's where she was working. I was on sick call that night. A bunch of us had a real case of the flu or whatever, and I had been on twenty-four-hour sick call. It's the only time I ever reported sick in Vietnam. I never reported sick afterwards because it was terrifying waking at quarter of six in the morning with this incredible thud and crunching metal like a bad car accident, but the metal was crunching, and then deathly, deathly quiet. That's what I will never forget... the eeriness of this explosion going off, and then it was deadly quiet and you knew something bad had happened.

Then the alarm went off and the sergeant of the guard came around and he was banging on doors telling everybody to get into their bunker. That was the first time it had ever happened. I had been there from October to June so that was new. I was in bed and I thought I had been killed because I had been hit in the head and I didn't know what happened. A plaque that I had had on my wall had fallen off and hit me. I can remember being stunned, wondering if I was dead, not knowing how a dead person felt, trying to feel for blood and realizing I was alive and feeling like a fool. Then getting up and running to try to get to the bunker, not knowing what was going to happen. Then we heard that the hospital had been hit. Now we were all in night clothes and flak jackets and helmets walking up to see the destruction of the unit and it was then that we heard that Sharon was dead, and I couldn't believe it. I can remember I was coughing and saying, "Well, now they'll know we're not safe anymore," because I knew they wouldn't be able to keep the news of a nurse being killed quiet in America. I used to write home and my parents would write back, or my family and my husband would say it's been quiet in Vietnam. I didn't know who was reporting the war, but we weren't quiet. I knew that they couldn't keep the news of a nurse dying quiet, and sure enough they couldn't. They made arrangements for the whole staff to be able to call home that night and I called to my parents' house because I knew my husband was traveling to their house. He was going to be getting out of the service soon and we were going to be moving to Boston, and I missed him. I kept telling my parents we had three minutes—"Mom, you've got to understand I'm okay." There were restrictions on what you could say and you couldn't tell people where you were, but

I sounded like death warmed over because I had a bad cold. All I said for three minutes was, "You've got to understand I'm okay," and that's it. It was after I called that the news broke in the United States and my mother thought that I was trying to tell her something, and my husband at the time, who was traveling, was distraught because all he had heard was a nurse was killed from Chu Lai, so I called back that next night and talked with him.

I don't remember a whole lot after that. I still have in my mind's eye the unit that was hit. Several Vietnamese people were killed. To this day, I want to say maybe four or five but I'm not sure, and isn't that sad that we don't even know? I have no recollection of them rebuilding the unit. That happened I think June 8 and in July I was assigned to the Vietnamese unit and I was very upset about that. That is my recollection of Sharon being killed. Again, I was angry because I knew she didn't hurt enough. She still thought that we were doing something good, and I knew that I had become not such a nice person, that probably I should have been the one, and I don't know if I'm alone in that, but I was so ashamed of those feelings I didn't talk about them all those years.

The guys, the male nurses in their hooch, two of them that I remember exactly, if they had not been on duty they would have been seriously injured. Shrapnel came through the roof through their beds, and all of a sudden you realize this isn't a joke. I don't know who's making up the rules back in the United States, but somebody doesn't know what they're talking about.

As a society we haven't learned very much. That really makes me very sad. I have two boys, one is nineteen-and-a-half and one is twenty-one and I have been asked many times in the past would I want them to serve or would they go to

Canada, would I support that? I think America is a great country. I think that we have a responsibility as men and women to defend our country, to know about it and to defend it, and I think that everybody has that right, not just poor people or minorities or people that need money for education as I did, I think everybody has that responsibility. If we took that responsibility and everybody had to serve, we would certainly look at the way we handled things for the military a little bit differently than we do now. We just think, "Well, they're going to take care of it," and that was the mindset in Vietnam. "Oh, they're doing their thing over there," that it's not going to impact us, and that's a fallacy.

When I first, I say, came out of the closet I never considered myself a veteran until my whole life was falling apart. I could no longer practice nursing, I didn't know why. I was afraid of everything, and I was in counseling for a long period of time. That was very difficult because there were very few places that knew what to do with women who were coming and saying, "We have problems and it's affecting our lives." We were held up to male standards for any kind of disability ratings. I was told a number of times early on, well I didn't serve in combat, what was my problem? I would just shut down. I didn't know what my problem was, maybe I'm just crazy. Yet, just like there's a male response for everything in life, so there is a female response, and it's not good or bad, or right or wrong, it's different. I think that the female response has certainly been to explore a lot more with Vietnam veterans.

We said we wanted to be recognized that we served in Vietnam. Through those efforts early on, we came to appreciate just how dismissed were the women veterans that preceded us from both World War II and Korea. When we were on duty, acting as nurses, I really felt like we were treated as queens or as angels. I mean, the guys really respected us, I felt, and treated us well. Step out of that role and you were a piece of meat, and that was always very difficult for me. I was an Irish Catholic girl, I was young, I was not used to men treating me that way, and I would wrestle with it. I mean, I told off more than one senior officer because he was out of line and always wondering what were the repercussions going to be because he was the senior officer? Would I be charged with insubordination? Could I be court-martialed because of it? I thought, what were they going to do, send me to Vietnam, dress me in a funny green uniform, keep me away for a year? What else could happen? That was my mindset and that developed stronger and stronger the longer I was in 'Nam.

Sometimes the GIs just adored you, and at times that was difficult, because that wasn't who we were. I certainly am not worthy of being adored by anybody. I did the best that I could. There was a mindset that they wanted you. It was like their fantasy that you were supposed to fill, although it was always unspoken. You never knew what was going on. I was a twenty-one, twenty-two-year-old young kid that had led a very sheltered life who all of a sudden was really in the muck right up to my neck, just trying to hold on. Just trying to hold on. We had stupid rules, like we didn't allow swearing in front of ourselves. In intensive care when the guys would wake up, we didn't allow them to swear because we were ladies, and when I think of it, I'm a lot more colorful in my language today than I was then. It's so absurd, but I thought, "No, lady, you didn't swear around ladies because that's where I came from." You didn't swear around ladies, and I don't know how we went through the war that way, without swearing. I've come a long way. Poor Tom when he was crying out for the bed pan, when he would say "I got to take a sheet," somebody would try to say "Tom, that's not right." This guy was dying, he had head wounds and everything else, and we're correcting his language. Excuse me! I think he had every right to say that, plus a few other rights. But, it was our way, I think, of holding on to something that doesn't make sense thirty years later.

I think the guys, especially the patients, really appreciated us, but you have to remember I worked in intensive care for about seven-and-a-half months, which was a long period of time. We were isolated. Our patients didn't have a lot of feedback for us. They were too sick and when they got a little better they were evacuated out because we had more coming in. After my experience there, I transferred to the Vietnamese ward and that's where I finished out my tour, about two-and-a-half months later, so I didn't have input from the GIs. Most of my experience or understanding of how the GIs treated the nurses was from my friends who worked on the medical or surgical wards that had GIs on them. We were one of the few hospitals that kept all the Vietnamese together once they left intensive care. I understand in other hospitals throughout Vietnam, they mixed them. We didn't. So I went from an isolated intensive care recovery unit to a Vietnamese unit. Other than the corpsmen and the nurses that I worked with, I didn't have a lot of exposure to the male patients. They appreciated the girls that worked there. They really did. I think it helped the guys get into the male/female thing. They tried to act better when there were women around. I think the guys appreciated us. They thought of us as sisters or mothers or girlfriends and acted appropriate once they realized they were in a safe place, for the most part. I had worked stateside with a lot of GIs and I mean there was inappropriate behavior sometimes, but for a lot of those guys it was the first time they were away from home. Sometimes they were just as scared as I was, and once you knew that, and you weren't looking for something else either, you just got along.

It seemed like the whole world's changed in that one year when I left. It was America as I had known and grown up. JFK had been killed. Martin Luther King had been killed in '68, and we lived through that, but we used to hear things overseas. The campus riots or the campus protesting and everything else didn't make sense to me. That was really not part of my world in the year that I left. And to come home, I had hoped that my husband was going to be able to meet me at the gate, and in fact, you had to come home to a closed base because people were being shot at. Several shots had been fired at military bases when people were walking off the planes from Vietnam, and you heard stories about people being spit on. The first time I had ever heard "baby killers" was when I was working. I worked at Massachusetts General here in Boston and people would talk about, "Oh, they're just baby killers," and I would be absolutely stunned. It was such a surreal world to come back to, with all of the sights and sounds and smells of a large city when you're used to this very small compound where it's the same thing day in and day out. That was surreal for me, coming home and living with somebody after being totally alone for the year. That was an adjustment, working in a new and strange place where you were not appreciated for the skills that you had. In fact, you were put in your place. I was put in my place more than once because what I did was not what nurses did. It stunned me because I had so many skills that I couldn't exercise anymore and I was being called on the carpet for it and reprimanded. Who did I think I was, did I think I was a doctor? That used to drive me crazy, but again, I was always sort of blinking my eyes at them, like what are you talking about? I learned very quickly if I told people I was a nurse in

Vietnam then I was an okay person, I was helping people. If I said I was just a woman in the military, there were not pleasant responses to that, and you just learned to keep your mouth shut. It was very difficult. I kept in touch with some of the people overseas for a few months and then I stopped. I was guilty for years over that. I felt like I was abandoning them, but it was so awful being back in a country that was protesting the war every night and labeling the men that were serving there, particularly the men that were serving there, as terrible people. Then the Jane Fondas coming out and making their statements. I certainly couldn't look at that as an intellectual, or stand back and get a perspective on it. It was hurtful, and you just learn to shut down. Even the people who loved me who, when I was reacting, would say, "Try not to think about it. Put it in the past. Nothing's going to hurt you now." So I never talked about my experiences. No one wanted to listen because when I talked I got very upset.

When I first came home, the My Lai trial was going on, and in fact, My Lai wasn't very far from Chu Lai where I was. It was like three villages out. Didn't mean anything to me. I didn't know that until I got home, but Calley was on trial and even my family said he wasn't really an American, and there was something wrong with him because Americans don't act like that. I said, "Excuse me, I don't think you know what it's about," that that wasn't the only occurrence, and I'm sure it happened in other wars. Oh no, Americans don't do that, it's only the enemy that does that, and I thought maybe I missed something. But I don't think so, and I hadn't even explored the anger that I felt. I was still guilty about being angry that Sharon died. The guys came home and you heard the stories about Vietnam veterans returning who were angry, hostile young men that had problems expressing themselves. People at home didn't know what to do with the women returning, having problems dealing with things, and so I just stopped. I just went into what I call now, like a pretend mode. I just wanted to believe everything that everybody told me, that if I didn't talk about it, it would go away. Then I would do the things I had been taught to do, be the good nurse, be the good wife, and keep the smile on my face and everything would be okay. But I didn't realize how much it affected me on such a profound level . . . on such a profound level. It took me years to find that out.

I think the responses are normal for what I went through. I think that we have to allow people that go into those situations, when they come back to their place of residence or their home, that there is a normal response pattern. It certainly wasn't allowed us, I think. I'm not in active counseling right now but I still touch base with her. I had shut down in a lot of ways. I used to have a huge circle of friends. Now I have a very small circle of friends. I'm a very quiet person. Stimulation seems to trigger a lot of things for dumb reasons that I don't understand. Large gatherings, large noises really just upset me, and I chose not to be upset anymore. I can't change them. It's not that they're doing anything wrong, whether it's family members or whatever, but it really does rattle me and I'm tired of spending so much energy trying to find out what's wrong. I just try to accept who I am now and remove myself from those people, and I really live a very quiet life.

Sometimes it's hard to say to myself that I did anything wrong, because I know that if I had had more nursing experience, maybe some of the guys would have lived . . . more of them would have lived. Yet I'm not God. There's a part of me that knows I did the best that I could with what I had at the time. I think we did an awesome job. It amazes me when I think back, and I see intensive care units today with their staffing and with their machines to help them. We had none of that. We would have four nurses, one nurse for the recovery, one nurse for medical surgical, one treatment nurse, and one charge nurse—the whole spiel for twelve hours at a time, and sometimes we worked nine- and eleven-day stretches. I don't know how physically we did it.

It's hard to remember all the death and destruction and not feel that maybe you could have done something more. I mean, intellectually I can hear my words and I know I did the best I could, but so much more was needed and we didn't have anything else to give. It was hard. There's just got to be a better way to solve your problems than fighting. I do a lot of thinking. We have such a war economy. Our whole economy is based on that, and if you say that to average people, they don't understand the implications of it. In order to change to a peace economy, the way it was between world wars where we didn't support such a huge military complex, people don't understand it and the cost that it will cost all of us. People will have to lose jobs, so you shift and make some others. People aren't willing to risk that. They don't want to have their own little worlds influenced, and that's why it keeps going on and on and on.

After World War II, when the troops came home, they hunkered down and started building society again, but they taught their children that it was important to speak out. I think that was one of the gifts that the World War II era, especially the vets, gave my generation. Our opinion was important and they solicited it, they encouraged it. I was born in 1946 and I think my generation was raised that way. My parent's generation wasn't raised that way. So when Vietnam came along and all of a sudden when you came home and people didn't want to hear it, well, I had already had twenty-one years' experience of another lifetime, another way of handling stress and talking about it. I thought that if people knew what was going on, then they wouldn't do it again. Well, it has been a big joy to learn that it doesn't work that way.

Born in Fall River, Massachusetts, Kathy Splinter was a 1967 graduate of the St. Luke's School of Nursing in New Bedford, Massachusetts. In

Vietnam she spent nine months of her tour in the 312th Evacuation Hospital and then at the 91st Evacuation Hospital, both in Chu Lai. The last part of her tour was in the Vietnamese ward, treating both South Vietnamese and captured Viet Cong prisoners. She married in 1968, and had two sons, Steven and David, now both college students. On her return from Vietnam she worked at Massachusetts General Hospital, and then in Los Angeles at Daniel Neemon Hospital as a surgical nurse. She returned to Massachusetts, worked as a school nurse and in social services. Divorced, and retired from nursing, in 1986 she bought and now manages Our Lady's Religious Store in Fall River, Massachusetts.

JUDY HARTLINE ELBRING
ARMY NURSE

Growing up, Judy Hartline Elbring heard war stories from her father, who had been a naval officer in World War II. After she graduated from college, she attended nursing school, joined the army, earned her degree in 1966, and immediately volunteered for Vietnam. She had nursing skills, there was a war on, and she felt she had to be there to help those who needed it. In February 1967, at twenty-four years of age, she was on her way to Vietnam. Her first stop was in Qui Nhon at the 67th Evacuation Hospital. She wore fatigues, and the casualties, now clean and starting to heal, wore blue pajamas while they waited for their trip out of Vietnam. That spring she and four other nurses were in Ahn Khe, the Central Highlands, where, Judy says, "It was definitely more warlike . . . and rocket and mortar attacks were fairly common." Only a few months later she was back in Qui Nhon in the POW ward. After a few weeks she was at the 2nd Surgical in Chu Lai on the South China Sea. She says, "Busy place. I spent long days working and long nights sitting up in the bunker while we were under red alert, attack

139

underway, thundering through our sleepless hours." Judy extended her tour for six months and was in Vietnam for the Tet Offensive. After returning home, now a senior captain, she "reupped" for another tour that took her to the 95th Evacuation Hospital in Danang, where she cared for her wounded brother, John, a helicopter pilot with the marines.

Largely, I went to nursing school so I could go to Vietnam. I needed the job that would get me into the war. I know that sounds absolutely and utterly amazing, but the stories that I had heard my father tell made it sound like it was very exciting. It was a chance to contribute, it was very patriotic, it was an American thing to do, and it was something that I could do now. I couldn't do it as a soldier, but I could do it as a nurse. That was why I went to nursing school. The nurses were all volunteers. We didn't have to go. But I wanted to go. The army subsidized my education, they paid for my time there, and I paid them back with three years of my service.

My dad really didn't try to talk me out of it. He really didn't. My dad thought it was noble, I think. He thought it was noble that I would go. My mother, wow, my God, I mean, my mother had lost her brother in World War II. If World War II hadn't ended, my father was just about to die. He had volunteered for a suicide mission that I didn't learn of until a lot of years later. My mother kind of got resigned about my going, and just figured that if that's what I was going to do, then she wasn't going to be able to stop me. I was headstrong. I could give the illusion that I was pretty much going along with the program, but no, I always had my own agenda. I don't think I've ever said that before. I don't see how they stood it. I mean, I'm older now and I have children. I don't see how my parents stood it. I don't see how they were quiet about it.

I did my basic training at Fort Sam Houston in San Antonio, Texas, where everyone in the medical went. So I did my basic training there, got my uniform there, used to run around behind the buildings to try to avoid seeing people who might salute me because I wasn't sure how a salute actually worked. A lot of us used to trail around behind the buildings trying to avoid the enlisted men that wanted to salute us, because we felt embarrassed. We didn't know what we were doing. After Fort Sam I got assigned to Fort Gordon, Georgia. I hated it. The day I arrived I walked into the chief nurse's office and made a request for transfer. She said, "You can't do that this soon, you have to be here three weeks." Three weeks later I went to her office and I requested Vietnam and about four weeks later I got it. That was 1966.

Vietnam was still that thing, way over there. Largely, it seemed to be advisors. Largely, what they seemed to need was nurses not so much for combat, but more to take care of the men who were already there performing some sort of—I call it stagnate duty—just where they were. To be whatever the back-up support was for the very few people I believed were out in the field that were actually supporting local forces to learn how to fight off communism—a worthy enough goal. That wasn't the way it was at all. I didn't know we weren't really prepared. Part of basic training, they had a mock-up village and we were to look at the village. Of course, basically, Vietnam was being taught based on what they had learned out of the conflict in the '50s. That was Korea, which didn't really apply, but it was the most recent war and apparently they always teach the newest war from the previous one.

They talked about things like not to pick up anything, that anything could be booby-trapped. Not to take a baby if it was handed to us because the baby might be booby-trapped. Not to

kick any cans because they could be booby-trapped. We were
warned about booby-traps everywhere. We were shown a village and they said some of the village was likely to be underground, and there would be pongee sticks [poisoned stakes in
the ground], but I kept thinking the whole time we were there
training, that it was like summer camp. It didn't make any
sense. I wasn't going to be in any villages where there were
pongee sticks and blowing-up babies. I didn't think I was getting prepared for that. I'll tell you, though, the day we arrived,
oh God. We went in a chartered aircraft, so all of the flight at-
tendants had their little perky red, white, and blue uniforms
and we're all sitting in our steadily enlarging drained bodies, in
our greens. We stepped off the airplane. And right away when
the door opened, the air conditioners stopped and the hot hit. I
thought, "What did I sign up for, what did I say I'd do?" We
started to walk out. It smelled bad, it was dirty, it was dusty,
and I saw a comic book lying on the tarmac. I started to bend
over to pick up the comic book and one of the other—I think
there were four nurses with all of the other men that were there,
one of the nurses shrieked at me—"That could be booby-
trapped, don't pick that up." And it hit me, suddenly, that I had
actually said I would do this, that I had gone. It was hot, it was
sticky, it was smelly, it was dangerous, there were things that
were booby-trapped, everything was green and dust and fences
and wire and noise, and I thought what a fool I'd been. This
didn't look like an adventure to me—this looked very serious.

In February, 1967, we came in at Long Binh. That was where
all of the nurses came in to be reassigned. We were issued our
fatigues and issued our boots and issued all of the stuff for jungle war we didn't have before. We met with the chief nurse in-
country and discussed where we wanted to go for our
assignments. Who knew? I didn't know. So it didn't make any

difference to me. I was assigned to the 67th Evac in Qui Nhon but that still didn't mean anything to me. Apparently it was II Corps, North. It was coastal. It was supposed to be relatively safe. It was a huge hospital, all things considered. It was supposed to have been a hangar and apparently General Westmoreland had come through there because there was an airfield and said rather than another hangar, we need a hospital because this is a good drop place for patients. So that was why it had been formed in February, 1966. When I got there, they had what they called a DEROS hump. DEROS, Date Estimated Return from Over Seas. Everybody from Vietnam knows what a DEROS is, that's the day you go home.

When everybody left the states, we were all brand new, and now we had these huge hospital wards. They were giant wards. God, how many people? I suppose there must have been sixty to eighty men in each of the wards. These were supposed to have been hangars, so they had huge high ceilings. The men all had their blue pajamas on by then, and they had their bandages on by then. It didn't look like war. It looked like just taking care of patients in a hospital. It didn't look like anything that was particularly dangerous or special and everyone said how safe Danang was, and we could go out walking in the village if we wanted to. We'd go out walking along the beach. We'd go out to the leper colony. Everything seemed to be very safe. It didn't feel like a war, so I lulled myself into thinking that this was a very safe place.

Then when they realized they had a DEROS hump and everybody that had come in February, 1967 was going to be leaving in February of 1968, they started to disperse us to various places. They took five of us and moved us to the Central Highlands, to An Khe, to open up a clearing company. So the five of us, and two or three doctors, a handful of corpsmen and a couple of administrative officers, in a truck, thank you, driving up Highway 1, which began to feel a lot more like being in a very strange place. We drove up to An Khe. We created a hospital. A clearing station. It's an aid station with nurses, and doctors and corpsmen. The marines had been there, and I guess when the marines leave they take everything with them. They even took the light fixtures. There was nothing, just these stripped-out buildings and tents. We had patients already waiting for us. A lot of village patients. A lot of local people were coming in then. More than I'd ever seen before. And the casualties started coming in. They weren't all neatly dressed in blue pajamas and nice white bandages. They were a mess. That was the first time it started feeling real. We were busy all the time. There was always something to do, always something to do. There wasn't time to be scared. There wasn't time to feel fooled, there wasn't time to worry about anything except the immediate job at hand. Then, there were finally too many of us there that had all arrived at the same time and I got moved again.

We got the wounded straight in from the field, and we didn't keep them for very long. We would air evac them right back out again. An Khe was sitting on what they called the "golf course." The "golf course" was the largest heliport in the world at the time. Every single kind of helicopter you could imagine was there. There were plenty of ways to get people in and get people out, so we were just kind of a way station.

Those guys were coming in straight from the field. Dustoffs brought them in. Wherever they'd been wounded, they were coming into us first. There were battalion aid stations, but it was like all rules were off. See, in the other kinds of wars, at least from everything I had to learn from all the various schools, there were lines. There was the forward edge of the battle. Reading early American history, or early British history, when

everyone would line up with their guns and shoot in a very orderly way and then step back and the next one would come and
then you knew where the lines were and this was behind and
that was in front. It wasn't like that. There wasn't a behind or an
in-front. It just *was*. An Khe, the 616th, was completely surrounded by what they called the *green line.* Literally they had
destroyed the foliage around the outside of it, and there were
guard towers, and we were an island. We were isolated. Hong
Kong Mountain came up the back end of An Khe and that's
where the radio tower was. Our little hospital was right at the
bottom of Hong Kong Mountain, and then this giant helipad
which of course was a pure invitation to be blown up. It took
fire all the time. We spent a lot of time in the bunkers.

We worked seven to seven. We did twelve-hour shifts because there weren't very many of us and there was plenty to
do. We'd quit at seven at night, grab something to eat, go to
sleep, because somewhere around ten, eleven, twelve o'clock,
the sirens would start for the red alert and we'd see the tracer
bullets going overhead and we'd go and sit in the bunkers. I
learned very fast the deal with sitting in the bunkers when I
was the first. It was not to be the first one in because that's
where the rats lived. So I got smart very quickly, and I would
doodle a little bit in putting on my flak jacket and my helmet,
and I'd let somebody else be first into the bunker and let them
chase the rats out. Then we'd sit in the bunker, pretty much all
night long. The all clear would sound around four or five in the
morning. We'd go out, we'd sleep for another hour, and then
go back on duty.

I don't think I ever felt constrained in terms of medical
treatment. We pretty much always had everything we needed.
It wasn't like the old *M.A.S.H.* series where they were con-
stantly running out of things. Re-supply was not a hard thing.

The Philippines weren't all that far away, but there were a lot of areas where there wasn't any fighting, close enough to Vietnam that we could always get supplies. That wasn't a problem. No, I never felt constraint in how I treated.

There are four categories of triage. I knew the theory of triage. The first ones are the most lightly wounded and they can wait because they're so lightly wounded and they might be able to help, or they just require some kind of quick bandaging. The second-stage ones need a little bit more help but they're definitely survivable and if you work on them quickly they're going to be fine and they might even be able to help. The third category are badly wounded, salvageable, and you got to work on them now. They bump everybody else out of the way when they come in. The fourth is the expectant. They're not expected to live, and they're not going to be treated. They're going to be put off to the side and they're going to die. I wasn't ready for that. That was just a theory. I wasn't ready for seeing those kids with holes in their heads and brains coming out of their heads, and that they were going to die. I wasn't prepared to look in a man's face and know that he wasn't going to make it, and know that I knew it, and he didn't know it yet. I wasn't ready for that. I don't know that there's any preparation for that. I can feel the feelings in me now as I talk about it. There was no time for those feelings then. There was no time for it. We just had to do what we had to do. To see a kid who's not that much younger than I am. He's my brother's age, and some of them are younger. They're eighteen and nineteen years old, and they're kids and they're skinny and they've been in the jungle too long and they haven't eaten well and the bones in their face show, and their uniforms are dirty and they smell bad, and now they're going to die. Now they're going to die. I remember after we were through work and had done all we needed to do, there would always be a few of them that were behind a curtain in the area where we used to keep them. It was off at the end of the one of the wards and we had a curtain drawn around it. I would go back there with them, and I would pet them until they died because, I was like their mother, their sister, their girlfriend. I was a round-eye. Even though they didn't know I was there, I knew I was there. I would stay with them until they died, because too many of them died alone, and that's not right. That's just not right. I didn't tell anybody about any of this stuff when I first got back. I didn't know how to tell anybody. I was afraid if I told people, that I would just start crying and I would never stop. I would never stop. I don't remember their names. I don't remember any of their names. I don't even know that I knew some of their names. I don't think I did.

It's too many names to remember. It was too many. When I finally went to the Wall, it was at the dedication of the Women's Memorial. I had never been there. I found the place in the Wall when I was there in Vietnam. It goes on and on. It's the biggest part of the Wall, 1967, 1968. It's huge. Tet was then. Tet was toward the end of my tour. I was in a different place then, too.

It always seemed strange that there would be a separation of officers and enlisted, but there was. There was an officer's club. There was drinking. There was always a lot of drinking. I got drunk. I don't know, maybe four or five times and I didn't like it, I didn't like it. So, drinking wasn't a way out. Flying? Flying was a way out. I don't think I'll ever forget the 229th Assault Helicopter Battalion at the first place in Qui Nhon. They were 1st Air Cav, and Charlie 229th used to remain overnight. The pilots would come in for hot showers in the hospital. A lot of warrant officers, a lot of young kids. They were so young. Some of them were younger than I was and they were piloting

aircraft around. Of course maybe they could look at me and
say I was too young to be a nurse, but these kids.... They were
normally stationed much farther north, up in Khe Sanh and
up in some other areas. They would offer rides, and I took
them up on it. I went riding around the country, anytime, anywhere I could. I've been in helicopters and fixed wing, and Chinooks and the big Sikorskis. They even would let me fly
sometimes. There's no trick to it once you're up there. It's a
bigger deal to try to hold them steady, but it's no trick once
you're up there, and then I would use the radio when we'd
come in. They would tell me what to say when we were going,
and they would say, "You talk on the radio, the guys will never
believe who I've got with me." So I would, I would. I would talk
and call in, and I always felt like the representative round-eye.
This is like your sister coming in here, this is somebody who
will look familiar to you. I had long hair and I wore it in a braid,
and I asked my mother to send me some colored yarn and I
would braid it in my hair but not for on-duty. When I was off-
duty I'd swing my braid over my shoulder with the yarn running through it and wear earrings and perfume and I would go
out riding in the helicopters and I would be the American girl.
I always felt like I was kind of a representative for everybody
that couldn't be there and that I would be the familiar girl. I'd
be somebody they could look at and I would look like home.
Nothing else did. But *I* would look like home.

I didn't think of it as a burden. See, that's what's so funny
about some of the things that I did then that seemed like such
right things to be doing and the dangers that I'm sure I was in.
I don't know why I never went down, but I didn't. On the helicopter it was a real place. Vietnam wasn't a real place. It never
felt completely real to me. It was like being in a movie sometimes. Does that make any sense? From the helicopter I could

watch what was going on, and it was like not being part of it. I went on combat assaults with people and I rode in the Charlie. Charlie is the commanding control helicopter that would fly above, and watch what was going on down below. I rode in the Delta ships, which were the gun ships that had mounted rockets on the side of the Hueys, and I would fly them. They had places they had chosen as practice targets, and I would fly and fire rockets at the targets, and take flybys. There was a part of me that wasn't a nurse at all when I was there. I was on a high adventure, doing things I would never have a chance to do anywhere else. I was running away from home and doing all the stuff I wasn't supposed to do. That's the part that doesn't fit in with being a nurse. That's the part that was harder for me to tell people because it didn't make sense to them. I began to see the reports that were coming back about how awful the war looked. When I saw it from the newscast in the living room standpoint, I thought, "I can't believe that I did all of those things." Why did I think this was a huge adventure punctuated by some of the stark terror we felt when they were marching rockets up the beach at us and we could hear them exploding, as they were trying to sight on where we were, and we could hear them getting closer and closer and closer? That was scary. A navy fuel dump got blown up one night. Everything in the hospital fell down. We had those glass IV bottles hanging from little bent nails that were on the ceiling. Everything jumped down and fell, and that was the beginning of Tet. That wasn't the one incident that did it, but that was at the very start of it.

I was in my fourth place. I was in 2nd Surgical in Chu Lai, and I felt like such a veteran. I could speak some Vietnamese by then. I traveled all over the country. I had gone from just south of the DMZ, all the way down to the Mekong Delta, all the way from east to west, I knew what it looked like in the

mountains. I knew what it looked in the coast. In 1967 it was a
beautiful country, by the way. It was very hard to believe there
was a war going on because it wasn't falling down. It wasn't
full of holes. It didn't look like anything that a movie ever
looked like in war. It didn't look like that. It was beautiful. It
was absolutely beautiful. I could see why the French made re-
sorts out of some of the areas. It was exquisite, and it didn't
look like a combat zone. I got to meet a lot of the people in the
villages. We weren't supposed to, but I did.

We'd go out and do medical missionary work in the villages.
We'd give immunizations, we'd bandage wounds, we'd go
take care of the people in the village. Sometimes I was the first
American woman that they had ever seen. There's a funny
thing with the kids. Now my arms I don't think are terribly
hairy, but they're much hairier than Vietnamese, who have
maybe twelve hairs on their whole body, and the little kids
would come up and they'd pet my arms when I'd go into the
villages. It wasn't like a war at all. It was like being especially
privileged to be invited into a completely different way of life
than any that I knew.

It was a good benefit. We did a lot of good work, and then we
did a lot of horrible things. I remember the night that a nearby
village had been Napalmed, and some of the people were sent
to us to take care of, and it was Americans that had dropped
Napalm on the village. It was an accident, it wasn't their target,
but that didn't matter to the people that were hurt. I remember,
in particular, I was assigned to take care of this baby. Just a
baby and he was burned everywhere. He wasn't going to live.
I was to debreed his wounds and cut away the dead tissue
around the edges of the wound. It seemed pointless to me to do
that, so rather than hurting him as he was dying, it was much
better just to hold him. I didn't treat him, I just held him, and

he died. That's the first time I can remember I was cleaning up after something we Americans did. This was a baby and this baby had nothing to do with the war. The children didn't have anything to do with the war. If any mother ever booby-trapped her child, it wasn't the child that was asking to do it, it wasn't the child's fault. It was never the children's fault. They were really the innocent ones, and the kids that were over there, our guys that were over there, they weren't a lot older. They were kids too.

Part of it was a big adventure I had gone there to have. Interspersed with flying was this awful reality of seeing our guys. I never did understand what was going on. I barely understand now and I've studied it more. I took care of the people that were immediately in front of me and did what was needed to be done medically. That part was easy. In its own way, that part was easy. Hurt is hurt, a bandage is a bandage. Bleeding? Stop bleeding. All of that, that made sense. But not some of the reasons behind it, and the longer I was there, the more I got to know some people from intelligence, and I started to hear some of the things that they talked about that were going on. I remember one day I witnessed some of it. We had heard the stories that sometimes if they had captured someone and they wanted information and they had more than one person, they had two or three people, they would take them all up into a helicopter and then, to make the point that they wanted them to speak and tell the truth about whatever piece of intelligence it was they were trying to gather, they would push one of them out of the helicopter, and then the other two would talk very readily. I heard that and thought that can't be so, we wouldn't do that, that's not something that we would do. One day we had a man, he had some kind of belly wound. He was Vietnamese, I don't know if he was North or South or VC or what he was—it didn't make any difference. He was wounded, and he had been brought in and he was bleeding from his belly. We had put a tube down his nose into his belly to start removing some of the blood, and we had hung blood to let the blood drip into him because he was losing a great deal of blood. One of the guys that was interrogating him told him that they were going to suck all the blood out of him, they weren't going to give him any more blood, and they were going to drain him dry of blood. Now he told him this in Vietnamese through an interpreter so I didn't know what it was but I saw the man get more scared and more scared. I finally said, "What are you doing, what are you doing? What are you doing to this man?" That was when one of them pulled me aside and said, well, this was accepted interrogation technique and they needed to do it, and I said, "Not here you don't, not once they're a patient you don't. When they're a patient and they're wounded, they're not for you to hurt anymore, they've been hurt. Now we take care of them," and I got my first taste of some of the lies, some of what wasn't true. I always thought we were the good guys. We weren't always the good guys.

I'd have my uniform on when I came home. That was how we had to travel. My sister had her flowers on, and as we embraced, people came over to us and spit on me and pushed me and called me baby killer and called me names, and I looked at my sister to see if she felt that way too. She didn't. I saw her and she saw me. Suddenly she was the only friendly face in the crowd. There was no one to talk to about this. In all my time it has only been in the last four years that I've had any contact with women veterans. No time during any of the rest of my nursing career, my anesthesia career, or since then, have I ever talked. There was no one to tell. Now I can talk to the guys. I feel like I have something special and there's something that we share. But we don't fully share, because their position was very different from mine, so I hadn't talked about any of this.

I finally went to the Wall. I went during the dedication of the Women's Memorial. I hadn't been before. I'd been in Washington before, but it hadn't been created yet. I'd only just heard about it. I really didn't know what to expect. When we got there, it was evening, and not very many people around. I didn't know it was that big. Somehow to see everybody's name, and that they belonged to somebody.... I knew some of the names on there would be people I had taken care of, even if I didn't know what their names were, their name was on there. It starts small in the 1950s, just a very small part of the Wall because there weren't that many, and it gets so huge, in 1967, 1968, 1969—so many people died. The size of it, the length of it, I had no idea. It was seeing the names so carefully carved out. So much neater and cleaner than any of them died. I don't know if that makes sense. It was almost too neat, almost too precise, almost too lined up. It somehow can't reflect the horror of holding a young man while he dies. It just can't. It's not the same. I looked at it and I wondered, because all the other monuments seemed to be glorious somehow, a general on a horse and the hooves raised, or a sword raised in battle, or something that has a feeling of victory, of we're right, or, you know, or we will prevail, might, strength, all the rest of it. But the Wall doesn't look like that at all. The Wall looks like all the guys who ever died, all the women who ever died, doing what the general has the sword in his hand that's supposed to be the glory thing, and that's not what it looks like. It looks like names carved out. It's a big tombstone. That's all it is. It's just a giant tombstone, with all of the names on it, and there are too many.

The ones I worry about now, because I can feel what it is for me to finally be saying some of what's true for me, I worry about all the women who aren't talking about it yet. There are a lot of women who aren't home yet. A lot of women. I didn't know I wasn't home until I went to that dedication of the Women's Memorial. As we were walking in this parade, which was as much the people who lined the streets as it was a parade, a lot of guys in pieces of uniforms, because a lot of men still just wear pieces of their uniforms, said "welcome home." I didn't realize until then that I hadn't been welcomed home. I didn't think I needed a parade. I didn't think I needed acknowledgment. I was just a nurse. That really is how I felt about it. I was just a nurse. I did my duty as I needed to do my duty. I even had a good time when I had a good time in my off times, but what I didn't get was that I hadn't been welcomed home, and if that's important for me, it's got to be important for other women too. I had no idea this was still affecting me. I had no idea that not saying anything could carry this long a toll on me, on anyone, and I'm not the only one. The part that scares me is, how many women are sitting on their anger, are sitting on their grief, are sitting on their sadness?

I sat on my mine for so long. I mean, one of the things I would hope that this would do is that it would open up for the women a pathway to come home again, a pathway to say, yeah, I was there and I was scared part of the time and I had adventures part of the time, and it was terrible watching your children die, it was awful. Mr. and Mrs. America, Mr. and Mrs. congresspersons, all of the people who declared the wars, it was terrible watching your children die. You have no idea what that looks like. If you did, you wouldn't have another war. You would not send the finest off to be killed. You just wouldn't.

The only ones you can send off to die are the young. You've got to take someone who's all charged up at eighteen and nineteen and twenty and wanting to go out and see the world and kill the enemy and do the things I'm supposed to do and do it for the right and the good and whatever reasons that they give. They're the only ones you can get to do it, the only ones that you can convince. You can't send somebody older than that and put a gun in their hand and tell them to go do that, they won't. They won't. Not if they've seen it. They won't do it.

My brother and sister and I were very close in age. We're only three years apart, the three of us. We're the World War II babies, 1942, 1943, and 1945. My baby brother decided to go into the marine corps. He went through flight school, he went through all of the flight training, decided on helicopters and when my time was up in September of 1969, he got his orders. I'd been paying enough attention by then to know that less than 50 percent of marine helicopter pilots made it back, and I didn't know what I could do, but I thought I do know my brother, and if he's hurt, I'm going to be there. I will always be in a safer place than he is, always. A funny little side story. When I got back from the first tour, there had been hepatitis and plague and an epidemic in the village right outside of Chu Lai. We had lots and lots and lots of admissions, and even though we worked very hard to try to keep everything from getting cross-contaminated, many of us did pick up hepatitis anyway. When I came back from the first tour, I had actually gone to Washington. D.C., to see the surgeon general to ask why, when I had re-upped for six months to stay in-country, why my orders had been changed. I figured I knew the place and I could speak some of the language and I wasn't bothered by being there. I wanted to know. My last stop was to see my brother in Pensacola where he was finishing up his flight training, and that was where the hepatitis really blossomed and I wound up in the naval hospital. My brother came to see me every day for two months. Every day, and I thought if there was ever anything that I could do I would support him, and then there was this. So that when he got his orders, I knew that's exactly what I was going to do. I was a senior captain. I had a second tour relative in country. I'd have my choice of locations and I would get myself stationed as close as I could to where he was and that whenever anything happened to him, if anything did, and I thought the odds were that it would, that I'd be able to take care of him. That was a gift that I could give my parents, and his wife.

They sent me back. He was in Phu Bai and they were closing down the 85th, but in Danang, the 95th Evac was still open. It wasn't that far away, so I requested Danang. I talked to my commanding officer within hours of the time that I arrived and said my brother was a marine, he was in country, he was in the north and if anything ever happened I wanted his permission to be able to fly to him. My brother talked to his CO and actually, I'm the one that exacted the promise from his commanding officer, that if anything ever happened I wanted to be notified, and I would be there.

I'm an attractive woman. It's my brother. I'd play any card I had. Any card. I did it on purpose. I figured that would get me what I wanted. That was it. I don't mind playing that card. The CO was a man, I knew I could appeal to him. He used to have reasons to come to Danang because the squadron headquarters were in Danang and he would always choose my brother as a co-pilot so there would be an excuse to stop by the hospital to see me. That was fine with me. I didn't care what it took, as long as I had an immediate and direct line to what I wanted out of this.

My brother was doing an extraction in Cambodia where, of course, we weren't. We weren't in Laos either, we weren't in a lot of places, but he was, and he was shot down. One of the men was killed and he was injured and the rest of the men were injured, and because it was late enough at night, they flew him back into the army hospital at Phu Bai. His CO called me and said he was sending a chopper for me, and they did. When I got to my brother, he still was not cleaned up from the field, he was still bloody and dirty, he had a chest tube in, and he was bloody and messy and awful. But I got to do what I went there for. I got to take care of him. I got to clean him up, and wipe the blood and the dirt off of him, and get him put into those nice blue pajamas where he would be safe and where he would have nice white bandages. I sat down with him, and we wrote a letter to my parents, and to his wife and I had us put words on the same page so they would know that everything was all right. When the chest tube was removed four days later, he was supposed to be air evaced into the navy chain, because marines go through the navy. He was supposed to have flown out to the hospital ship, so I made friends with the registrar, and I had the registrar change his air evac tag to read my hospital, and I got him air evaced to the 95th. When he got there I hand-picked the ward that I wanted him to go on, and who it was I wanted to have take care of him. This was just before Christmas, and I flew back to his squadron and I got all his stuff and dragged as much out as I could so that he would have it to go with him. Then I got him air evaced out to Japan. If a marine stayed out of country thirty days or more, he could not be sent back to Vietnam. I couldn't save anybody else, but I could get my brother out, and he didn't have to come back. Believe me, the rest of the tour was easy after that. It was easy. For a long time my brother didn't know why I went back. I didn't tell him. I worked all of this around it. I only told him a few years ago.

Men were not a problem, not really. I always felt so in charge, so in control. I loved that there were fifty thousand men to one of me. There was something that was very satisfying about that. I used to do a lot of entertaining whenever I could. I had a ukulele and I had a guitar and I even found an old pump organ. I used to go out with one of the chaplains to the drop zones to give services, and I would play this little pump organ with my feet and wear my hair down. I always wore my hair down when I was out in the field so that they would know that there was a woman there. I felt respected. I felt honored. It was never really a problem among the men. I felt treated very specially. I was treated as a sister, more than anything else. I was treated as a big sister. I never had trouble with any of the men. No. I was a million miles from home. I figured my father couldn't find out what I was doing in a combat zone. Sure I had romance, hand-picked, and some very special men. Yeah, I did. And I enjoyed it. There was something about the danger, about the send-off, about the wondering if we had tomorrow, that I didn't want to wait.

There was one kid I will never get out of my mind. It was in my second tour. Remember it was Danang and I was supervisor of the hospital then, at night, and we got a chopper load in. I don't know why this kid stands out in my mind, but he does. He was filthy dirty, covered with mud, covered with blood. His neck was exposed, his shirt had been opened down and he had holes in his neck and they weren't bleeding. He was yellow-purple-white, that awful color of death, and because he made it that far we always tried to revive anybody who made it that far. I remember putting the mask on his face and squeezing the bag, and seeing the air come out the holes in his neck and knowing that we couldn't do anything, that he was gone. Suddenly, he was every one of them, all wrapped up into this one boy. This one boy. I had never felt so helpless in my life. There was nothing to do, there was no bleeding to stop, there was no hole to fill, there was no way to make the air go into him, there was no way to make his heart start pumping again. I can still see his face. His face always stays with me. His dark hair and just a little bit onto his forehead, and that awful pale skin, and his face, except for being pale, looking completely normal, completely uninjured. Everything was from his neck down, all of these holes, and he was dead. When we touched him he was cold. There was nothing we could do. He stays with me. I don't know why he stays with me, but he does. He comes back in my dreams. They aren't always horrible dreams either, but they're helpless dreams in a way. They're all of the things that I can't do anything about. For some reason, this boy holds them all for me. It's his face that stays with me. I have a thousand faces in my mind, ten thousand faces in my mind, but his stays the strongest.

I would love to be somebody's good dream. Oh God. Oh God, wouldn't that be wonderful? Wouldn't that be wonderful. That would be wonderful. I hope I am somebody's good dream. I'd be very proud to be somebody's good dream. Wow.

Judy Hartline Elbring was born in 1942 in Evanston, Illinois. As a child she lived in Florida and when World War II ended and her father, a naval

officer, returned home, her family moved to Riverside, Illinois. Next they went to Paducah, Kentucky, in 1957, where Judy completed high school at Paducah Tilghman in 1960. At DePauw University in Greencastle, Indiana, she earned her BA degree in psychology, zoology, and chemistry in three-and-a-half years, graduating in 1964. She says, "I bummed around Europe for several months after graduation until I realized that my precious degree qualified me to do no particular job." So, because of her father, and her desire to go to Vietnam, she studied nursing in St. Louis at the Washington University School of Nursing. She joined the WACs and was a private first class. She graduated as a 2nd Lieutenant in the Army Nurse Corps and was in Vietnam by February, 1967. After returning home in 1969, she says, "I slipped quietly out of the war." She started work on a Master's degree at Vanderbilt University in Nashville, Tennessee. At night she ran a surgical intensive care unit. Compared to nursing in a war zone, "Civilian nursing was boring, filled with discouraging paperwork, peppered with little nursing care." Six months later she left the program and by the fall of 1971, she was back in St. Louis in the Barnes School of Nurse Anesthesia. Two years later she was a Nurse Practitioner in Anesthesia. She met a fellow student in the program and they married. He had been a surgical nurse in the air force who had difficulty coping with his return to civilian life. In time his desire for speed caught up to him and he became yet another casualty of war when his small plane crashed in the mountains of New Mexico. Judy, six weeks pregnant at the time, saw her life change again. Over the next few years, her son Scott in tow, she worked at different Army Reserve hospitals until 1980 when she unexpectedly renewed her friendship with Bill Elbring, a former college boyfriend, then divorced. They decided the time was right for them to be together. They married, began their new life in Indiana and went to the West Coast where they now live in Penngrove, California. Together they formed Life Partners in 1989, serving as relationship teachers coaching people to create healthy relationships with each other.

THEY ALSO SERVED

BOBBIE KEITH
SECRETARY, USAID
ARMED FORCES TELEVISION
WEATHER GIRL

Bobbie Keith was a secretary for the U.S. Agency for International Development (USAID). She worked at the Mondial Hotel USAID Annex in Cholon, the Chinese section of Saigon. She lived on Nguyen Hue Street in downtown Saigon, halfway across the city from her office. Only nineteen in 1967, her life took an unusual turn when, sitting in a cafeteria, a colonel offered Bobbie a job as a weather girl for Armed Forces Television. Soon Keith was appearing on television nightly, sometimes in a bikini, and doing humorous stunts to entertain the troops. She became a favorite of the GIs and she regularly visited troops in the field at their base camps, sometimes coming under fire during an attack. Bobbie Keith was a welcome breath of fresh air who lifted the troop's spirits everywhere she went.

I'm an army brat. We had been posted to Japan. I was studying at Sophia University in Tokyo when my father was reassigned to Fort Monroe, Kona Kip Quarters in Hampton, Virginia. When we returned to the states it sort of put me in a state of limbo about what was I going to do next because I had left Japan with my studies behind me. I ran into two girlfriends. There was a recruitment campaign going on in 1966, about going to Vietnam, and at that point, I think you're either going to demonstrate against the war or you're going to join it. Since both my parents served in World War II—my mother was a navy nurse—I felt it was something that I needed to do as part of the family. Every member of my family—there's no one that didn't serve. It's a very patriotic family. I don't like the stringent hierarchy of the military, so I preferred going as a civilian. It just hit us that they were recruiting for USAID. Two of my girlfriends and myself wound up in this same place after the three of us talked each other into going.

For our training, we had sensitivity awareness programming about the population, the diversity of the Vietnamese people, their cultural background, their history, their religious backgrounds. We learned why we were there and about our commitment for being there and the meaning of the domino theory. We had a little bit of propaganda and indoctrination. We had Vietnamese language training, what they call a survival course, so when you arrived you could maybe take a taxi, order food, do something simple. It wasn't anything complicated. Many of our people went on to one year intensive language training.

We were nervous, we were excited, it was an adventure, it was a learning experience. We all wanted to be there. We all wanted to participate in what we thought was right. We were trained to believe the commitment to be there was right. It's only years later that maybe you start doubting it. You don't really face that reality until you see it. The reality really didn't hit until Tet, and that's when you start really thinking, "Oh, this is dangerous."

The first thing that hits you in Saigon is the very oppressive heat. It is really oppressive. I was soaking wet before I left the airport, I mean, I was sopped. Then, there is the odor. You do see the combat uniforms. You do see the camouflage everywhere. It is very noticeable that you see a lot more men than you do women. You see smaller people than I was accustomed to seeing because the Vietnamese are a little shorter in stature than we are. You could smell fuel, you could smell *ngoc mam*—a fish odor—and not the most pleasant odor. It was just a potpourri of different things that you experience.

The first hotel I was assigned to, the Astor Hotel on Nguyen Hue Street, was primitive. We didn't have hot water. We didn't have air conditioning. We had small little cots with no mattresses that one person could barely fit in. We had all of our meals out. There were no facilities to eat in the hotel. They were extremely small rooms, extremely small toilets. You could sit on the toilet and take a shower at the same time and a small ripple of water would come out and it would be cold. It wasn't very pleasant. But a few months later I was reassigned to another hotel, the Excelsior Hotel, which was a step up. I had a bathtub, a balcony, air conditioning, and a bed.

I was assigned to work at the Mondale Hotel, which is out near Cholon in the commodity import program, which was responsible for bringing in the products for staples. Mine was strictly secretarial, strictly clerical duties, and, to be very honest, they weren't that demanding. But we worked long, hard hours. We had signed contracts to be available to the needs of the service, which meant we worked whenever it was necessary: Saturdays, Sundays, late at night, whatever.

I became the weather girl actually by a fluke. I think it could have been anybody. I just happened to be at a place where I was spotted. They were looking for someone to do the weather show. I was with my girlfriends when Colonel Mash came over to the table, and said, "You look like a weather girl." We were laughing. When he talked about the audition, we didn't think it was serious. They asked if I would come out and audition. I had not intended to do it, but when my friends teased me so much I decided I was going to try anyway. They were teasing me about even thinking about going out and doing it, like I couldn't do it, or you're crazy. "Why do you want to get involved in that, you have a job?" Well it was a job, but it was a volunteer job. I mean, you don't get paid for doing the weather show. I was quite surprised that I passed the audition. That's when it started.

When I first started doing the weather I was nineteen. I sat down in front of the camera. They had me sitting on a stool, until they recognized that sitting on a stool you couldn't point or do anything. You couldn't turn your head and look at the temperatures. You were just being like a robot perhaps, on a stool. So the next thing they did was give me a wand, so I could play with this little wand and point until I finally graduated to the point where I could walk around and do the show. To find the weather, all I had to do was pull the ticker tapes, or go into the press room and find out what the different temperatures were. If we didn't know what the different temperatures were, we just kind of surmised what the temperature might be up in Plaiku, for example. Because you know it's always hot, you know it's going to be between 80 and 90 degrees and maybe even 101. And to be very honest, since it was always hot, I don't think people focused on whether it was 100 or 103 degrees, so we had a little bit of fudge room.

I was never an entertainer. I don't think you could say the show was entertaining, although it became that way. They wanted a female. We did do crazy stunts on the weather show. We tried to make it light and funny and not serious because people didn't pay attention to the temperatures. We called attention to people's home towns. The guys would write in and say, "Well, mention my hometown down in Memphis, Tennessee, one day and say the temperature back home in Memphis is..." I flew around the studio on a broomstick for Halloween one time. I arrived on a motorcycle one time. I was put in a box one time, like the Houdini-type style, and elevated up. They threw a lot of buckets of water on me when I announced rain. People thought that was funny. I wore different costumes. One time they painted the temperatures on my body in a bikini.

In Saigon, women already had a profile. Any woman there, because there weren't enough of us, had a profile. There were very few of us. So we were already designated round-eye, and everywhere you went as a woman, profile or no profile, I mean, TV or no TV, you were afforded a courtesy by the men because we were there. Once I was given the profile because of the TV, then the invitations came in to do the handshake tours and go out and visit the troops, and that kind of elevated my profile. It put me more in a spotlight than maybe some of the women who didn't make the trips. I traveled out to the field by helicopter in most circumstances, and by different types of helicopters. Perhaps my favorite was visits to the 199th. The helicopter didn't have doors and could fly right over the tops of the trees. We'd start out in one place and go visit very small groups of the men out in the field and spend maybe thirty to forty-five minutes visiting two or three men, having a Coke, having a chat, and then get back in the helicopter and continue the cycle.

You could say they were called morale-boosting tours. I call
them handshake tours because you shake a lot of hands. That
was the term that we used. The different units would call into
the studio, talk to the studio, and arrange to have me visit.
They would say, "Could Bobbie come out please?" One example would be when they had so many casualties with the Rome
plows, not too far out of Saigon, they called in and said, "We
need Bobbie to come in and boost morale." So if you could say
that the presence of an American female boosted morale, I
think every female there boosted their morale, just by being
there. I think when females are out in a war zone, out in the
boonies, as such, that it brings a touch of home. Just the fact
that maybe when I was wearing White Shoulders the guys
would say, "Ah gee, that smells so familiar, my girlfriend wears
that," or "Gee, you remind me of my sister," or "Gee, you make
me homesick." It's bringing a touch of home to them. That
boosts morale.

The men make you feel good, because they're homesick, and
you can bring just the fragrance of the White Shoulders, to remind them of home, or make them smile. They were more curious about why I was there. They were very generous, very
sweet, very shy. I have to say the whole time I served in Vietnam I was never, never subjected to anything off-color, any harassment, it's like *au contraire*. The men were shy, they were
reticent, they often didn't know what to do with a woman out
in the field. They kind of looked at you, maybe put their head
down and not make eye contact, or they'd come over and smell
you. It was cute, it really was. Going out in the field I felt as if I
was treated like everybody's kid sister, or I replaced the one
they left behind, their loved ones. I was never treated like a sex
object. Even when I saw the pin-ups posted on some of the
hooches on visits, and they asked for me, I don't think that's

what they thought of me. I think that I just gave them a touch of home and that's what they were looking for. I think it's what you call PR, public relations. The people were writing and asking for me to visit. I didn't expect it. I think if you can bring a touch of home to remote places, many women did this. I'm not the only woman. We had a lot of Red Cross workers go out to remote places. We had USO entertainers go out. Not all of the women were able to go to remote places. I got to them because I was not restricted in what I did.

You would start at a headquarters or base camp where they were headquartered, and from there you would get on the helicopters and go out to the different smaller camps, so I usually didn't know some of the names of the places.

We could hit three to four camps in one day sometimes. Break, and maybe when they were having stand-downs, have lunch with the troops out in the field, or go to where they were having a stand-down. One of my favorite things was to serve chow in the mess halls because then you could just say, "May I serve you?" and it would give a big shock for them to look up and see a woman serving chow in a chow line.

Going out on the handshake tours was always muddy or dusty. The climate never really changed, so you'd be in muck, mud, wet or dry, and flaky with a crust of dust on your skin all the time because of the weather. The heat was very oppressive, so you were never able to cool off, although I think one of the funniest things I saw was a cold beer being thrown out of a helicopter. Actually, it wasn't a beer either, they were throwing Cokes down at us one time to have something cold to drink because we were way out in the middle of nowhere and it was hot, and they flew by and just threw the cans out. It's kind of cute.

My 1st Cav jacket is my favorite memento, it really is. It means more to me than anything else I brought back from Vietnam because the Cav gave it to me with the Cav patch and the Blue Max patch during my visit. They put my name on it, of course no rank, so I don't mind being the "civilian unknown other," whatever, no rank. But it started a tradition that when I wore it, people would give me the patches of the units I went to visit, so all the patches went on the jacket. The 1st Cavalry, if I understand correctly, is the oldest division we have in the United States. Their history goes way back to the times when they were doing the charges with the sabers on horses. They had a very large group of the Cav in Vietnam. They happened to be the ones to make me an honorary Sky Trooper in Vietnam and continued supporting me in the United States because they made me an honorary member of the 1st Cavalry Division Association in the United States, which is a very big honor, so I really appreciate the fact that I'm supported by them.

Saigon was not under siege, not like in a war zone, but rockets came into the city. They had bombings in the city and a lot of sabotage by the Viet Cong. Things did go on because we always had a curfew to protect us. And I was in places that were attacked too.

That's why Tet is kind of really burned into my memory. We went out during Tet. In fact I was with a girlfriend. We went out to deliver boxed lunches to the engineer battalion that was redoing the wires, the telephone things, all the communications that had been destroyed from the attack or the battles that were going on. The battles were still going on because they were flushing out the Viet Cong from the city. So the battles weren't over just in one or two days, they kind of continued. Our first checkpoint there was by a Viet Cong hidden in the theater. They started shooting out of the theater so we wound up behind the big water barrel barricades. You'd think that would scare us enough to stop the journey, but we got back in the jeep and we continued our little journey. At one of our stops we were just getting the boxed lunches out of the jeep and Viet Cong had been hiding in the garbage.... I mean, a big heap of garbage that was in the area. They were just firing off rounds, hitting the guys in the poles that were up there, so we wound up under the jeep. And then they decided to take us home, that maybe that was a bit too much for us two women.

The fear doesn't hit you. The emotions don't hit you. To be very honest, I don't think I felt anything during my time there. You bury everything, you really do. We had a very bad habit of ignoring the war. We didn't talk about it, we didn't want to give validity to it, we ignored it. Right in the middle of it, we ignored it. But when you come home or you see the traveling Wall, and you go to Washington, D.C., and you see the Wall with all the names on the black granite, the inscriptions, then it hits home. Then the impact really is overwhelming. When I was there in Vietnam.... no, there wasn't an impact—not until I saw the Wall.

I was on an all-night trip down in the Delta where a guy was blown up in front of my face. It was an accident, and I really shouldn't talk about it, because people don't need to know. I mean, there were accidents that happened in the war, not every single death was combat related. Accidents happened, and it was a freak accident, and I just happened to be standing there when it happened. I think probably everyone who was in the country was in danger because of the way the Viet Cong acted. Their tactics of terror, the indiscriminate rocketing of the cities, the sabotaging. They would put satchel mines inside of a night club, for example, and you could be in the night club at the time it was blown up. Or, when our BOQs, bachelor officers' quarters, and BEQs, bachelor enlisted quarters, in Saigon were blown up, and the American Embassy was blown up too.

My office building was hit and blown, just the first floor, part of the first floor, but not destroyed.

As an army brat, and my father serving in the military all his life and my mother serving as a nurse, if I hadn't gone or done something, as their daughter, because I'm not their son, the family would have been disappointed. I'd rather be part of history and see history or be there than to watch it on TV and not really know what happened.

I don't think that any of us started doubting our methods or doubting the domino theory or doubting the commitment or why we were there until after Tet, and that's when you begin to wonder, when the casualties get higher and higher and you go, "Why are we doing this, why are we losing so many men, for what reason?" And you do start thinking, is it worth it?

We lost women too, thank you, because a lot of people don't know how many women we lost. Inscribed on the Wall in Washington, D.C., there are eight names of women who were in the military service. However, we lost fifty-five civilian women in Vietnam, some because of direct combat, directly related to combat situations, like when the Viet Cong attacked the Lipsorium and killed the missionary women or when the American Embassy was bombed and a woman was killed.

I think I was very fortunate that my time frame in Vietnam, I didn't see the problems that they talk about now, that maybe happened in the 70s where they had the psychedelic drugs and they had the problems of the men indulging in recreational drugs. I mean, how do you explain it? I didn't see that. I don't think the men indulged in that. My generation, the group of men that were over during my time frame, I have a lot more admiration and respect for them. They were maybe, perhaps more put together, but they were all very young and shy at the same time. When I went out and visited with the troops, we actually really didn't talk much about the war. I think perhaps people did start doubting it, like myself, after Tet. You doubt it when your buddy gets killed, or you know that people have lost their lives. You begin to question the reason why the people have lost their lives. But in all honesty, to be polite to me, I think they ignored it when I was on a visit with them.

I like to have good memories, I don't want to have the sad memories. One good memory and bad memory was Commander Quary would go down to the Delta and pick up the men from the LST boats and the PBR boats, bring them back to Tan Son Nhut, board a C-141 troop cargo, or a C-142, whatever it was, and we would board that great big troop cargo plane and fly out to Con Son Island for a one-day R&R. It was a paradise of a white sandy beach . . . and you're safe. We would have that one day R&R, a cookout on the beach, maybe a steak barbecue, maybe some cold beer, cold Cokes, whatever. Then, you'd watch the faces of the men and when it came to noon, you'd have to get back on that C-141 and the men would have to go back to the war, so it's both a good memory and a bad memory. Because you always sit and you wonder, "Okay, the men went back to war, and I went back to presumably the safety of Saigon, right?" Because I wasn't in the war, I wasn't in combat, and so you sit and you always wonder what happens.

As a woman living in Vietnam I don't know how perhaps the other women might feel, but for myself personally, I never wanted to get attached to someone. I had already lost people during Tet, so I, perhaps by the time Tet was over, and the May Offensive as well, I had lost three loved ones. I didn't want to attach myself to anyone again, because of the fear of losing them again. The reality of life over there was you don't want to get attached to people because of the fear of losing them. Because once it's happened once, you don't know if it's going to happen again, if you're going to lose someone. So I remained very celibate.

I had a lot of exciting trips. Truly, every single trip I made was very special. I would never in a million years think I would have been invited to visit the ships, if you want to say the Gulf of Tonkin, out in the South China Sea. Because my mother having been a navy nurse I was truly excited to go out and visit the fleet of the ships and go to the *USS Enterprise*. They were so generous and so nice to give me the captain's cabin to stay in. Of course, when we went around the ship, we did a radio show and we did a closed-circuit TV show on board. Everywhere I went around the ship I had one man in front of me and one man behind me and I think that's for what you call decorum or modesty. There were men stationed outside the quarters I stayed in, close to that side, although I didn't think I needed to fear anything, I really don't. I never feared that anything would ever happen to me because of men.

I think if I were to say anything about Vietnam, I would probably say had I not had the naiveté of youth, like so many of the men, I wouldn't have survived. Because the naiveté of youth kind of gives you the feeling like nothing is real, nothing is permanent, you can survive it. You have that resiliency, and you have that mindset with youth. I truly don't think I could do it today. I truly do not think so. I was only able to do it then because of my age. The most difficult thing is when you realize how indiscriminate war is. That was the reality that I brought home . . . war is very indiscriminate. It doesn't matter who it hits, it doesn't care who it hits. Your soldiers are victims of it, and then your civilian population—they are victims of it, too. That was the reality that came, that hit me.

When you leave the country, and you're out of the country, you go, "Wow—what a relief to be away from it all." I felt so relieved, it's like a weight had been lifted from my shoulders. Then you bury it, and you escape it and you bury it deep, deep, deep, until you see the Wall. I'm glad I served. I'm proud that I served. Lots of women were there. Women have always been there. I don't think the men realize how many women were there in the diversity in their numbers, and they quite frankly don't even know how to handle the women today. It's more "in" for the men to go hug a nurse, but when they find out that you're an "unknown other" or a civilian, they don't know what to do.

What I remember is in the almost three years of being in Vietnam, I never heard a bird sing. Never, not once.

Born in Winthrop, Massachusetts, Bobbie Keith calls herself an army brat, and rightly so. Both parents served in World War II. Her mother was a navy nurse and her father landed in Normandy on D-Day. He

served in the Korean War and Vietnam, and today lies buried in Arlington National Cemetery. She grew up in five countries and seven states, graduated from high school at Grant Air Force Base in Japan and attended Sophia University in Tokyo for two years. When her father's next assignment took him to Fort Monroe, Virginia, she returned home. She joined USAID with two friends because she thought, "We should do something for our country and for the adventure of it all." Starting in November, 1966, Keith had extensive training in what to expect in case of terrorism, and she learned "street survival Vietnamese," such as taking a taxi and bargaining at the market. She arrived in Vietnam in April, 1967, soon became the weather girl on AFVN-TV, and the rest is history. In November, 1969, Keith resigned from USAID. In 1975 she went to work for the Department of State Foreign Service and continued the life she began as an army brat, working in a different country every two years: Germany, Jordan, France, Turkey, Colombia, Morocco. She returned to the United States in 1988, discovered the Wall, and became a "yellow hat volunteer" at the Wall. Bobbie Keith says, "Seeing the Wall for the first time, and having the memories of Vietnam flood your mind, is an overwhelming experience. I would never have thought it cathartic, but when people say the Wall is a catharsis, I now believe it, as life in Vietnam was a roller-coaster ride of emotions." She took a government buyout in 1994 and retired to be with her parents in South Florida, where she still lives and sails as often as the weather permits.

CHRIS NOEL
ENTERTAINER

For five years, from 1966–1971, each night of the week, Chris Noel broadcast "A Date with Chris," on Armed Forces Radio around the world. Soon the show became very popular with the troops in Saigon, and Washington asked her to go there to visit the troops. Though already a young Hollywood star, she had a call to duty . . . visit Vietnam and entertain the troops. Once there, she flew to bases all over the country. She sang, danced, played rock 'n' roll on her portable phonograph, and dispensed warmth and good cheer everywhere she went. One Christmas in Vietnam, Bob Hope introduced her as "Chris Noel . . . Miss Christmas." Broadcasting in English to American troops in South Vietnam, she was America's answer to Hanoi Hannah, the voice of North Vietnam.

I had a fabulous life in Hollywood. I was one of the Golden Girls, I was under contract to MGM. I was appearing in lots of movies opposite Steve McQueen and Elvis Presley. I had

wonderful boyfriends. Hugh O'Brien was one of my boyfriends. I had very handsome boyfriends, a beautiful, beautiful glamorous life.

It all started in 1965, Christmas. I went with Governor
Brown and various Hollywood celebrities to the hospitals in
San Diego and San Francisco, Balboa Hospital. I went into
what is called the "gangrene ward" of double and triple amputees, and I saw Sandy Koufax throw a ball to one of the
guys who had one arm and he caught that ball. The guys
would smile when they saw the girls, myself and my room-
mate Eileen O'Neil. Some of the guys sat there and they were
very depressed and very angry and wouldn't respond at all.
When I left, that day changed my life. I saw the destruction of
war. My boyfriend was in Vietnam with Bob Hope and I
thought to myself, so this is what war really is like, and I
wanted to go to Vietnam.

The most amazing thing is—whoever would have dreamt
it?—I had this desire in my soul that if I had an opportunity to
go to Vietnam that I would go and do whatever it was that I
could do. If it was to do nothing but stand there and smile, I
would do it, whatever it was. I just felt compelled. And all of a
sudden, out of the blue, came an opportunity. I auditioned for
a radio show on Armed Forces Radio. It was called Armed
Forces Radio and Television Service. At that time in Hollywood the shows were taped and then they were put on 33⅓
records and sent throughout the free world. Of course, in Vietnam my show became extremely popular. The show was
played in Antarctica and on ships at sea and various remote
places. I played music and did interviews with many celebrities. I made dedications to the guys that sent me letters from
Vietnam and asked me if I would actually send a letter back to
them and a picture and if I would make a dedication. So I

would go, "This is for you guys at the First Infantry Division, the Big Red One, and especially to you, Robert, and First Lieutenant James Smith. I'd like to dedicate this song to you fighting men in Southeast Asia, 'We Got to Get Out of This Place.'" I became the first woman since World War II to broadcast, have my own show.

I had requested to the people at Armed Forces Radio that I would really like to go to Vietnam. I wondered if Bob Hope would let me go with him, and the answer came back, "No, the Bob Hope show is already booked up." I mean, he had big celebrities on his show and I was just an upcoming actress. Even though I had been on Bob Hope's shows before as a deb star and as one of the girls most likely to succeed in Hollywood and that sort of the thing, they just felt as though they had their show already booked. They had it down to the penny as to how they were going to spend their money and where their money came from. The next thing I knew I received a telegram from Washington asking if I, Chris Noel, would go over and help build morale of the troops, and I went, "Yes, yes, yes, yes." I was asked by the Department of Defense to go to Vietnam and help build the morale. It was great, I liked doing what I did, because when I went to Vietnam, I went over by myself, and an escort officer would meet me and he would be my escort. Because I was by myself I got to go everywhere. I could go out and visit two six-men teams of special forces, I could go into the Montagnard villages, I could watch them train the Cambodians, I could go as far south to where they brought in the ARVN, actually where they brought in the prisoners of war, and they had them bound and were taking them over to an island. I saw all kinds of things when I was in Vietnam.

When I arrived, I remember great anticipation and I don't

think anything really hit me until the door of the aircraft opened and I walked out, and I'm looking around and I see uniforms everywhere, and guns. An officer came up to me and said, "Welcome to Vietnam, Miss Noel, I'm your escort officer." We went into Saigon and we were in a vehicle that had things over the windows so that grenades couldn't be thrown in. I went right in. I mean, I didn't have to wait for any kind of inspections or anything like that, I was able to go right in. Everywhere I looked, of course, were people on mopeds and little bikes and it was really just such a change from America. The culture is so entirely different.

I can imagine what it must have been like for each one of these guys on an individual level going into Vietnam. See, in this war, the guys didn't go in as units where they already knew each other and came back that same way. It was really lonely going over by yourself and coming home by yourself, a very, very lonely existence. The first thing they did, they took me to a Vietnamese hotel and I sat there in that hotel room. They were coming back to get me for dinner and then start to show me what I was going to be doing. The first thing I said is, "I'm not staying here," and they said, "What do you mean you're not staying here?" I said, "Because everybody is Vietnamese. I'm the only American here. I can't speak to anybody and I'm not going to stay. I came here to be with the troops, I didn't come here to stay in a Vietnamese hotel," and so they said, "Well, okay." They took me immediately out and they found another place for me where I could stay with the military. They took me up to the top of something where we had something to eat and you could see what looked like fireworks, and I said, "What is all of that?" They said, "Well, it's firing," and that was the beginning of my hearing what the sound of firing sounded like from mortars and actually seeing fireworks in the sky. It was incredible to be sitting in what appeared like a safe city on the top floor, and watch the fireworks.

I would travel throughout the scope of South Vietnam by helicopter to various fire bases, and LZs, landing zones. When it was time to go further up north, I'd go by different kind of air-craft. Sometimes I would stay in the tents with guys and I'd have my little space. I'll never forget the first time that hap-pened. I really had to go to the bathroom, I have to tell you, and I had no idea where it was, but I could see someone walking back and forth in the light, and I could hear guys going "uh-huh" all night long, that sort of little noises, and I had to go so bad. So I took my little wash-up basin, and then of course I was afraid to even step anywhere because I didn't know if I was going to step on a rat or what because I had mosquito netting all around. It was pretty tough being a woman when you needed to be alone. So I traveled the entire scope of Vietnam and stood there and stared at them and they stared at me and I went, "Oh no, I've got to have something more to offer them than this," so I learned to sing.

When I first started traveling throughout South Vietnam it was called a handshake tour. I would shake hands with the guys and I had photographs and I'd sign them to them and then I'd start humming some songs and then singing a little bit here and there. I had a little record player, and I would play records, and I'd try to get the guys to dance with me. I'd sing along to the music, and then I learned songs that I could sing without music. I did whatever I could to try to make them laugh, and just feel normal for a few moments. I tried to get them to dance with me to some of the Top 40 music and then sing along to them, and then I'd sing some songs without music like, "Slow down, you move too fast/You've got to make the moment last/Just kicking down the cobblestones/Looking for love and feeling groovy."

I'd sing to them and I just tried to get them to laugh and to feel like normal human beings for a moment.

It must have worked because now all these years later, certain guys are inviting me to travel throughout the United States to come and see them. I'm not any more of a singer now than I was then, and it just doesn't seem to matter. We're growing old together and it's really kind of fun. I have a lot of—what I liked the best—a lot of men in my life, and that's good.

Probably the first time I actually heard incoming was when the rounds were coming in to where we were. I was told to run to a bunker and I didn't even know where one was. Another time I was in a little trailer one of the officers had let me have, and I was able to sleep in it that night. Of course whenever I got into my space to sleep I didn't get up for anything because the nighttime was very scary, and I didn't get up, I just stayed wherever I was planted. Early the next morning, I started hearing a BOOM, BOOM, and I went, "Uhhhh." I got underneath this little cot, and then I decided to put some clothes on and started dressing sitting down on the floor. Then finally I decided I'd better get out of there. It was the end of the cease fire, and we had started what's called harassment fire. Mortars are going out, but I didn't know that, so each new sound would be something that I had to learn what to expect. I was in sniper fire. I was on a little highway and we had about three jeeps and a sniper fired at us. I was actually thrown into, like, a little trench along the way. They were firing at all of us. Then after a while the sniper was pretty much all handled and they said it was safe that we could go again. When you're in the middle of the war, you forget where you are half the time. Any rock 'n' roll performer can attest to that, to wake up and go, "What city am I in?" That's the way it was in Vietnam. I remember it was at night, a helicopter was coming in to take me back off the mountaintop down to a more secure area. I remember the guys picking me up and they threw me into that chopper just like I was a sack of potatoes. I could hear fire hitting the helicopter. Whatever the noise was, I could hear it hitting the helicopter, and I was really happy to get out of there.

I went down in a helicopter. Of course, when you go down the hydraulic system is not working, and nothing is working. The hydraulic system went out, all the control lights went on and as soon as they went on, I knew we were in trouble. I saw them go on and I could see the guys were like really concerned. You have no idea when you tilt. And if those rotors hit the ground, the helicopter can go right up in flames. We just bumped real hard, and everybody was okay. The door gunners were probably more scared than anybody because I remember one of them right in front of me ripping the weapon off of the chopper and just slicing his hands in the process of trying to get it off. They were the ones that were scared, probably more so than I was. I felt that we were really very lucky and as soon as we landed the guys, the door gunners, formed a perimeter around us with the weapons they pulled off the helicopter. Out in the distance, believe it or not was a platoon coming to us because we went right down in a rice paddy next to a suspected VC village. The captain of the guys in the distance coming to save us went to school with me. That was pretty amazing. Because the next day he says, "My guys got you out of there," and I went, "Your guys?" He said, "Yeah." He said that was one of my platoons.

I never thought I was going to die in Vietnam, I never did. I just felt so protected. Now in today's lifetime, I could say that I really had some wonderful or several guardian angels around me, if one believes that way. I do. At that time I didn't, but obviously that's what it was. I mean, I had been in accidents on

the highways and stuff where I've sailed right through and
people all around me were wiped out. Things like that, and it's
almost like angels pick me up and move me because it's still
not my time. I mean, I could just name events that have happened right and left in my lifetime and I go, "Whew, thank you,
I guess this isn't the time."

There were a lot of times when I would say, "I don't know if
I'm ever going to do this again." Then there would be times
when I would say, "I've got to do this again," and they'd say,
"Will you ever come back again?" I'd go, "Yeah, I'll come when
nobody else wants to be here. I'll come in the middle of the
summer." Sometimes it was real intense. It was horrible sometimes. Horrible. Sometimes I would even say I don't want to go
to another veteran's reunion. Why? Because of all the emotions it brings up. I'm a highly emotional person, and I'm an
actor. It's just sometimes very difficult for me when I find out
that friends of mine had killed themselves or died from Agent
Orange or PTSD got them. So many of these fine men are gone.
They're gone. There are a lot of times I was sick. I would get
sick, from various things. That red dust just like near almost
killed me with bronchitis. I had food poisoning when I went to
the aircraft carrier *Ticonderoga*. I had food poisoning from the
night before. I was so violently ill and I had to get up and say to
someone, "I can't button my jacket. Can you button it for me?"
I tried to force myself to smile and be brave a lot of times when
I felt flat and didn't feel like it. I wasn't brave. I wasn't always
happy and for me to have to be the one to put the happy face on
to make everybody else feel better, sometimes it was not easy.
What made me continue to want to go to Vietnam? I would say
the look, the eyes of the men. The look in their eyes. I would see
all kinds of things. I would see sadness, I would see those that
were gone already. I've looked into the face of shell shock

where someone is just lying on a stretcher just staring straight and nothing moves. That is so scary. It was their smiles that told me that I made a difference. We all know we make a difference in people's lives. We have our choices, we can either make the difference in someone's life and make them happier or we can make them very, very sad. And I chose to make a difference in these men's lives by making them happy for a few moments. They in turn would give energy back to me that made me feel good and happy.

People didn't understand it when I'd say my kind of serenity was in Vietnam when I was sitting in the helicopter by the door, next to the door gunner. I'd be sitting there where I could look out, and no one could talk to me. I could put some makeup on if I wanted to and I could hear that tat-tat, you know, the sounds of the rudders, cho-cho, or whatever it is. But the sound of those rudders and the wind blowing and that was like a time of serenity for me. I loved helicopters.

My only fashion trend that I feel proud of, I guess you could say, is I took the miniskirt to Southeast Asia. Yes I did. And of course, the guys loved it because they got to see legs for a change. They very seldom ever saw any American girls, and then they got to actually see kneecaps and legs—ah—what we are fighting for! Then the bar girls loved the miniskirt. It was hysterical. There was an article that came out that said when Chris Noel left Vietnam, she left behind the image of the miniskirt and now the bar girls are wearing the miniskirts. I thought it was funny. I had them at the right length. I knew how to keep my knees together—my mama taught me that one—and I had on my go-go boots so I could jump in and out of those helicopters faster than the guys could. I was good! They probably wished I wasn't, but I was good!

In the field, I'd stand up on stages, on little bunkers. I didn't really dance. I'm not such a hot dancer. You just kind of move and sing some songs and go, "Hi." Everything you could think of just to get reactions and have the guys happy.

Once I remember I said, "Guys, what's wrong with him, what's wrong with that guy? What's happening?" They said he just got a Dear John letter and I said, "Really?" So I walked over to him and I said, "Hi." I said, "I'm Chris, what's your name?" and he told me. I said, "Can I sit next to you for a second?" And he said, "Yeah." I said, "I understand you got a Dear John letter." I said, "Let me tell you something she's not worth it. Don't let yourself get so bummed out over her because if she's going to leave you now, when you really need her, she'll leave you some other time. You'll find a great girl and when you go home, you'll be fine. So it will be a little lonely for you and you'll be lonely like some of these other guys, but you're going to be fine." I sat and talked to him, and I tried to do that. I tried to, whenever I had the moment or could see when someone was suffering, to take a little extra time.

Everything just goes together. It just seems like one giant trip. The interesting thing is to go from war to glamour. The glamour of premiers, and I was always going to premiers and glamorous parties. I was on the A-list and I really went to really fabulous events, and then go back to war again, and then go back to Hollywood and then back to war. That was what was so bizarre, and my personality started changing, let me tell you. I was no longer the pretty little starlet that just walked everywhere with a smile on her face. I remember before there was a really handsome guy that would always say to me, "Why are you always smiling?" and I'd say, "Because I'm happy."

I probably am not a very normal person today. And that's okay. I like being who I am today. I really went through a lot, and I've survived, I'm a very strong woman, but at the same time I might just start crying for any reason. I'm a Cancer, well, a moon child, so there's no telling where my mood swings will go.

Bob Hope would say, "Here's one of our most beautiful girls in Hollywood. Some of you will probably recognize her and she is combating Hanoi Hannah on the radio. I'd like to introduce to you Miss—from Hollywood, California, Miss Chris Noel!" I don't sound like Bob Hope, do I? You just go out there and do your shows and you'd be happy that you were alive. That's how I felt about it. Of course, it was the largest audience that I ever had in Vietnam. Boy I'll tell you, he could pack them in, and the stage was beautiful and fancy, and it was wonderful to have live musicians and so I just got up and I read something about, I don't know, some kind of Christmas poem that someone had given me the night before and I thought it was kind of cool so I read it to the audience to get them to have a laugh. He gave me a great introduction because he remembered me from shows that I had been on in Hollywood, so it was a very nice experience to be up on stage with him in Vietnam and it was entirely different from my other experiences. It was very show biz!

Hanoi Hannah was really part of the objective of putting me on the air, because as much passion as I had for what I did for America, she had for what she was doing for Hanoi, for the North Vietnamese. I understand there was more than one Hanoi Hannah, but the fact is that whomever it was could speak English very well, and was able to play some of our Top 40 music that our guys liked listening to. Then she would do the propaganda bit of trying to tear them down, tear down certain units by saying, "Spec 4 Ryan, you think that your wife is home patiently waiting for you? Little do you know that she is with your best friend Robert." Just tear people down in that manner, and the information would come from certain women in America that would feed it to them. We can all thank Jane Fonda and her friends for that. That's one of the reasons why Jane Fonda went to North Vietnam, because she was friends with the women and then she had women's groups back here in America who would delve up the information and stuff and they all would feed it back. I think she's a traitor to the United States of America. I think she has a lot of blood on her hands. And she didn't think anything that she did was wrong.

Even certain members of the press were quite aware of what I was doing and a lot of my headlines were "Chris Noel Combats Hanoi Hannah," "Green-eyed Blonde Combats Hanoi Hannah," "Hollywood Starlet Combats Hanoi Hannah." Supposedly part of my work was to be another female voice that would attract the GIs, the American fighting men, so they wouldn't be listening to Hanoi Hannah and the propaganda that would hurt them, turn around and hurt them. Hanoi Hannah could even tell them sometimes where certain units were heading, and where they were planning big battles. She would know the maneuvers and stuff, and say, "You think we don't know where you're going, you think we don't know this? We're sitting there waiting for you suckers." Oh, she was good.

I'm a very patriotic woman and I believe that if my country asked me to do something, I'd do it, no questions asked. A lot of these guys did exactly the same thing. And yes, if I were ever asked to do it again, what I did, I would say yes. By the way, I did put my life on the line, and I was not paid to go to Vietnam. I went as a volunteer because I was asked to, for no payment whatsoever. To me that is the height of volunteerism, when you're putting your life on the line. I was with those boys in the field. I had to stay that way. Whether we had all made the wrong decision or not, I could have been absolutely no value to them if I had stopped what I was doing, or if I had turned around and said, "Hey guys, we're all stupid, we shouldn't be here." I couldn't have helped them one iota. All I could do is to say, "Hang in there and be the best you can be, stay alive, and you're loved." But if I were asked to go today with what goes down with Clinton, no way. Why? First of all, as far as I'm concerned, he is the coward of the earth, draft dodger who knows nothing about the military. Wouldn't trust any move that he would make.

I never thought I was ever going to die in Vietnam. It didn't make any difference to me where I was. I just tried to always keep a very positive outlook while I was there, and if I was sick and throwing up and I'd just be sick and throw up and keep on trucking, and just being as brave and as strong as I knew how to be.

The first time it came up that I had a price on my head, was when someone said, "Chris, looks like you've got a price on your head now." I said, "Well, what does that mean?" "Well, it means that you have a price on your head of $10,000 for someone to kill you," and I go, "Why would anyone want to kill me?" "Well, they feel that if you were wiped out it would demoralize the troops and that it would be in their favor." I thought, "Okay," and then I heard it again and I said, "Are you sure? Oh, come on," naive little old thing that I was.

Actually, every time I came back from Vietnam, usually when I got into an airplane, I just slept. I'd get next to a window and I would sleep the entire flight back. I don't think I ate. I don't know if I ever even got up. All I know is, I just slept, slept, slept. As soon as I got home, all I did was sleep, sleep, sleep. That's basically what I did. Then as time went on, I noticed I wasn't the same. I wasn't the same happy, cheerful, young girl who left Florida, went to New York for modeling, went into commercials and then went to Hollywood to be in films. I was so different. I was deep. I was dark too. Very deep, and I stayed that way for a long time. I still am very deep, but at the same time, I can throw things off. I can laugh now and actually there are times when I feel like I have my youth back, believe it or not, where when I was really suffering, I felt like an old, old, old, old woman. I feel younger now than I did twenty years ago.

Most of Hollywood was totally against that war and Jane Fonda was real hot at that time. All of her friends believed like she did, and so here is this up-and-coming actress fighting for what I believed in, for the fighting man, and people didn't think like that. I was the outsider. I became the outsider. I had no intentions of abandoning my career. It just happened as time went on. I was no longer popular. People just didn't want the girl who worked in Vietnam to be in their films. What's really interesting is if you started asking the question to people who said they were against the war, there is not one single person that I have heard that said, "Yes, I spat on a Vietnam vet, yes, I threw something at them, yes, I called him names." They all say, "Well, I wasn't mad at him. I just didn't' think we should be in the war." Well, let me tell you something, they don't have enough courage to stand up to who they were then, because they were mean, they were horrible, and they created a malady in these guys and gals that hurt them. Some of them have gone to their death with the pain from it because even if you have a next-door neighbor who starts calling you names and starts egging your house and starts giving you a hard time, you're going to have a pretty miserable life. Having people do that when you just came back from seeing so many atrocities, coming back from your buddy having been wounded or another one die next to you with his blood and guts all over your face—you remember all of this stuff. Then you have people on the streets doing nothing but trying to tear your heart out—it's so pitiful.

I remember hearing this one woman say about me, "What? She was never in a movie. Just look at her, no way she was in a movie." Then I remember someone else say, "She was also in Vietnam." She said there weren't women in Vietnam, and I could hear everything. I could hear these women talking about me, and I went wow, you know, everywhere I go I can't really get away from it. I called the '70s my dead generation, or my dead decade. I just blocked it all out and pretended nothing ever happened and I just tried to live a life over it. Well, you can't live like that. Best thing to do is just go ahead and talk about it and get it over with, but no one wanted to talk then. The reason people are so interested in talking now is because there's so much space, there's not a whole lot of feelings involved like it was then, whether you were for or against the war. So all that space, and a whole generation of younger people have come along who are curious. And let's face it, the Vietnam War is history. I'm now a part of history, so now people want to hear little bits and pieces of history, where before they weren't interested in the truth and the reality at that time. They just weren't interested. They didn't want to hear it. I feel I made a difference in a lot of people's lives. They tell me I did. They come up to me today and tell me.

I have homeless shelters in three cities for disabled homeless American veterans. I founded the program. We're in our seventh year and we're doing very, very well. It took seven years to get the attention from the VA to even begin to help us. They did nothing for us but we certainly served the veterans that were at the VA when they came out of operations and stuff in hospitals and had nowhere to go. We helped a lot of them, and we still do. We now have a good relationship with the VA but it took all this time to build it, and frankly, the VA should be doing the work that I'm doing. Anyway, I shouldn't even have to. Some civilian woman who was in Vietnam taking care of all these homeless vets is something the government should be doing. But you either sit around and complain all you want about all the injustices in the world, or you decide to do something about it. This is what I chose to do.

Born in West Palm Beach, Florida, in 1941, Chris Noel became a model after graduating from Palm Beach High School. She then went to Hollywood and quickly joined the A-list of starlets, where she appeared in movies with Elvis Presley, Dennis Hopper, and Steve McQueen. She put her Hollywood career on hold during the years she entertained the troops. When she returned, she had difficulty finding regular work, be-

cause, she says, "Hollywood was hostile to me for my positive stance during the war." In the ten years after the war, she became drug dependent, suffered from severe depression and realized she, too, had post–traumatic stress disorder. However, she persevered, solved her problems, and kept working. In television she appeared in *My Three Sons, Perry Mason, China Beach, Bewitched, Burke's Law, The Tonight Show, What's My Line?* and *Merv Griffin.* She is a motivational speaker and the author of *A Matter of Survival—The War Jane Never Saw,* a book about her experiences in Vietnam. She is the founder and president of the Vetsville Cease Fire House Program. It is a nonprofit organization that supports three housing facilities for homeless and disabled vets and their families in Boynton Beach, Riviera Beach, and West Palm Beach, Florida. In 1999, Vetsville served more than six hundred veterans and their families with food, clothing, transportation, housing, and needed social services.

AMERICAN
RED CROSS

Susan Bradshaw McLean
Red Cross Donut Dolly

In 1969, at only twenty-one years of age, Susan McLean toured Europe and visited East Berlin. That trip changed her life. She saw communism first hand, and how people lived behind the Berlin Wall. In June 1970, after graduating from Longwood College in Virginia, she decided to do what she could to help in Vietnam. She entered the July, 1970 American Red Cross class for Supplemental Recreational Activities Overseas. After being trained in Saigon, she went to An Khe with the 4th Division, then on to temporary duty in Danang. She then became part of a new Red Cross unit at Quang Tri in I Corps, and finished her tour at the American base in Qui Nhon.

I know that everybody used to ask us why women went to Vietnam? "What's a nice girl like you doing in a place like this?" I think for me, it all started back in the summer of 1969 when I got to go to Europe with my college. I was on the European tour and having a grand time and having a lot of fun until we hit Berlin. We had our chance to go across Checkpoint Charlie and go into East Berlin. Even though we were only there one day, it was quite a day. You really got to see communism. You got to feel what it was like. You got to see the difference between East Berlin and West Berlin. We had friends in West Berlin and they had gotten me a date with a guy who had escaped from East Berlin, and to see what he had gone through just to have the freedom that we had and we took so much for granted, was quite an eye opener for me. So I had planned to go into the Vista program after graduating from college, but after seeing this communism and seeing what people were trying to fight against, I decided that I'd really like to do something to help the fight against communism.

The Red Cross Donut Dollies were volunteers. They had to be twenty-one to twenty-four, they had to be single and they had to be a college graduate, and they had to pass a pretty rigorous security clearance. The term came during World War II, when the girls in the Red Cross really did make donuts, and pass out donuts. The term just stuck. Our technical term was Supplemental Recreational Activities Overseas, so Donut Dollies sounded a lot better.

We were back in that "save the world" mode in the late sixties and early seventies. The guy that I was dating my senior year in college had already been to Vietnam, and he said that when he was in Vietnam he had seen Donut Dollies twice while he was there and he didn't even speak to them. He said it was such a shock that all they could do was stare at them, and he said that it gave the men a reason to get up in the morning. "If you really want to do something productive," he said, "today might be the day that the Donut Dollies come back." I said, "Well, what exactly did these Donut Dollies do?" And he said, "Talk." I said, "What else?" He said, "Oh, I don't know, but they just talked," and I said, "I could do that. I have finally found my job, I can go talk to guys. That sounds like something I could do."

I went to a teacher's college and teaching contracts were coming out, and I had applied to the Red Cross at the beginning of my senior year and hadn't heard anything. As the teaching contracts were coming out, I finally called the Red Cross and said, "I've got to know, I've either got to sign a teaching contract or I've got to get serious about this job." So it was Easter Sunday of 1970 and the Red Cross flew me to Atlanta, Georgia, and put me through rigorous interviews the next day, and after about seven or eight different interviews they offered me the job. It was tough telling my folks that this was the decision that I had made after graduating. My brother had gone to a military school and when he graduated he owed the military four years and they were sure he was going to Vietnam. He was really lucky, he got sent to Germany with the tank corps instead, so they thought the war was over for them. They never thought, and it never occurred to them, that their daughter would volunteer to go to Vietnam. Yes, they were definitely against it. Not just the safety part of it, but what would the neighbors say? What would the neighbors think? It's not what I was raised to do. It was the first time in my life I ever bucked society because being raised in the South, and being raised a lady, I went to a school where we were ladies, and we just did what our parents told us to do. But I felt so strongly about this that I decided that I really needed to do this.

We had to train first. We spent a month of training in Washington, D.C. Girls from all over the United States landed in Washington, D.C. We learned military procedures and we learned Red Cross procedures. We learned and learned. We had more shots. We went to the Pentagon and we just did a flurry of different types of activities for about a month in Washington. Then we left and flew to San Francisco, and we stayed there about three days near Travis Air Force Base getting ready to take off. I remember much more leaving Washington, because that's when I left my family. I was engaged at the time and that's when I left my fiancé. That to me was the biggest trauma. It was like, there's my mom, there's my dad, there's my fiancé, do I really want this door to close on this airplane? Back in those days, they let you actually let a guest walk down to the airplane with you. It was kind of like, "Either you guys need to get off the plane or she needs to get off the plane, but we've got to shut the door." It was a pretty traumatic experience, just having that door shut in Washington. By the time we got to California, I didn't know anybody, and I didn't particularly care that I was leaving California, but leaving D.C. was tough.

Arriving in Saigon in November, 1970, was one of those things where the door opens and the smell is just incredible. It's unlike anything you've ever smelled before or will smell or can smell. The blast of heat was incredible, and my first thought as I stood on the top of the steps was, "I think I should have listened to Mom this time. This is one I should have let Mom win." I knew I was in trouble. This was like nothing I'd ever experienced before. It got worse. It went from bad to worse. We got into Saigon, went to our hotels, had to lug up six flights of steps our sixty pounds of luggage that we were allowed. The sheets were dirty. They had already been used. They weren't clean and there was no water to drink. The geckos were on the ceiling, and I had never seen them. I was just amazed with these critters running all around. Even though I had traveled to Europe, I still was not anywhere near prepared for life as I was about to start experiencing it.

We were going to a party in Saigon and we were on a military bus. I remember as we were coming around the corner, the bus hit a Vietnamese, and I had never seen anybody hit by a vehicle before. We were screaming and yelling, and the bus driver didn't stop. We were going, "You just hit somebody and you didn't stop," and he said, "If we stop, there will be a riot." And I went, "He just hit somebody and we didn't stop," and then I knew the rules had changed. I knew things were really different.

As a Donut Dolly you had basically two choices. You could be a hostess in a recreation center and if you stayed in a rec center your job was to make sure the library was stocked, that there were arts and crafts materials, and that there were cold drinks on hand for the guys. You would put on one theme a day. It might be a Monte Carlo party, it might be a baseball theme, but they would have theme parties every day. Just try to make sure that you were like a hostess for this rec hall where the guys could drop in and spend some leisure time. I chose to do the forward areas, which meant I went out every day, usually by helicopter, sometimes by jeep, sometimes by tank, sometimes by convoy or ship or whatever. But we went out to the guys that couldn't come into the bases, so we went to the more remote areas of the country and put on recreational programs out there for them.

The guys used to laugh about the games, but there was nothing else to do. It was an ice breaker. It was fun. If you didn't play the games, they would just sit and stare because they could only ask you where you were from just so many times. It gave them a chance to laugh. It gave them a chance to think about something besides the war. It gave them a chance to have a little competition. It gave us a chance to interact. The programs usually lasted about an hour. Each one of the programs had a theme to it, and usually something like a Jeopardy game or flash cards, or at the end of the baseball cards we might have bat balls, at the end of another program we might have dart guns. Just games, just something different for an hour.

We didn't even think about safety. You just did it. It might be safe, it might not be safe. You might get in there and you might not get out. That was always a problem, a concern that we had too, that they couldn't come back and pick us up. The chopper pilots took really good care of us and they were neat guys. In fact, a lot of times they came in to get us when it wasn't safe for them, but they knew they wanted to get us off a fire base.

Things happened. You could hear it. You could see it. You could see the mortar rounds walking, they called it walking it in, you could see the mortars coming closer, the sound coming closer and closer. But we also had a lot of funny experiences. I remember the first time we went out it was raining and we were getting ready to land and all the guys were taking showers. They were standing out there taking showers. We had to go around in circles for awhile until they finished their showers. So, funny stories too.

Every day we would have something funny happen, because the guys in Vietnam were the funniest people. They had the best sense of humor. They were always doing really funny things, and we laughed a lot. We were either laughing or crying, there didn't seem to be any middle of the road, and we were either having a really terrific time or we were really right down there in the bottom of the pits. I think one of the funniest ones that comes to mind is the fact that we used to have trouble going to the bathroom in Vietnam because there were no bathrooms for girls on the bases. We finally got to this fire base that had a three header in it, and it was just like luxury to look at this outhouse that had three holes in it. It was so embarrassing that we had to ask a guard to go the bathroom with us. They would knock on the door, and they'd stick their head in, and then they'd have to stand guard while we went to the bathroom. This particular moment at the three header, the guard had knocked on the door and kind of glanced in, and I went in. I was getting ready to go to the bathroom and there was a gentlemen sitting at the end and he went, "I've died and gone to heaven." I came out the door, and I literally flattened the guard, I mean the door just hit the poor guard who was standing there. He had no clue I was coming out and I just went over him coming out of the bathroom. Bathroom stories were always a big one for the girls. It was tough, because we could be out on a fire base for hours and hours and hours and hours, and there was just no way for a girl to go to the bathroom.

Ginny—Virginia Kirsch—was my friend in training and even though we had only been together probably like forty days, people who were going to Vietnam bonded very quickly and very rapidly, and Ginny was a pretty special person. She was from Brooksfield, Ohio. Wonderful, very vivacious, very caring girl who came from a large family. She loved kids, was very religious, had already done her student teaching and had just decided that she really wanted to do something to help America. So she was one of the twenty-six girls that were in my training class.

I liked her sense of humor. She was funny. She was a really fun person. Plus we were bridge players. At night after training, a lot of us would get together and play bridge. She was always there for her friends, very fiercely protective of people and their rights. I grew up in the South where we just went, "Yes, ma'am and no, ma'am and just walk all over me, go ahead," and she didn't. She stood up for people's rights and she stood up for what she believed in. A perfect example of it was when I got engaged during training class and I came back with my diamond and I was so excited, but the Red Cross was not excited. They said, "This will not do. You're not going." And the rules said you had to be twenty-one to twenty-four, single, and a college graduate. Ginny went to bat for me; I was just going to go, "Okay, fine." I said I'm not going, or I'll give the diamond back or whatever, but Ginny went after them and she said, "Single is single, engaged is still single, and she's going and she's taking her diamond." It was kind of neat to see that more assertive personality. I took the diamond with me.

We lived in compounds that were supposed to be well guarded. They had fences and concertina wire around the compound and somehow this GI got through all of it and stabbed Ginny seven times. She was murdered in 1970 in Cu Chi about thirteen or fourteen days after we arrived in country, stabbed seven times in her sleep. She had never met the guy, and he managed to get in past the guards. Nobody knows why Ginny got stabbed and nobody knows why he did it. He went back to the states and he was found to be insane so he never had to stand trial. He spent the rest of his tour in a psychiatric hospital from what I understand, and then he was released with an honorable discharge and then he went on to kill again. So he's in prison now.

That was the worst experience. We used to talk about it during training. We knew that we could die, but we never knew we could be murdered, especially by the good guys, by the people that we were going over there to serve. I think she was in service to her country, and I think her name needs to be on the Wall. We were civilians and even though we went over—and the government asked us to go over—we had no rights. We were exposed to Agent Orange and we can't go to the doctors that know about Agent Orange. We had three girls that were killed in Vietnam and their names can't be on the Wall.

I watched Americans killing Americans. I watched mistakes that killed Americans. I watched Americans kill themselves. One of my friends succeeded, and one gentleman that was sitting next to me on a chopper tried to commit suicide in the helicopter. He tried to slide his way out of the helicopter when we were about 5,000 feet up. I had my seat belt on, and I just noticed that he was disappearing next to me. He was sitting there and the next thing he was slithering out. They had to leave the doors open on the helicopters so the door gunners could shoot. He was just kind of disappearing and he was standing on the skids of the helicopter and the door gunner got him. One of the pilots came back to help get him, and then ended up sitting on him until they could land. Back in those days they actually did come out with straitjackets and they took him off in a straitjacket. The guys were away from their family. They were away from their friends. They were bored. They were scared. They probably weren't all together before they came, a lot of them, and these conditions just made a bad situation even worse. Drugs and alcohol were a big factor.

The biggest movement that I saw was heading out towards Khe Sanh and there was an experience that I'll never forget. It was terrifying. We didn't know what was going on. We were in Quang Tri and all of a sudden they started canceling our stops. They were saying, guys aren't going to be there. The guys aren't going to be there. Then we just looked up and caravan after caravan, and convoys just started heading into Quang Tri and then heading out towards Khe Sanh. About five, six, seven times the normal amount of helicopters were coming in. Chinooks were coming in. Everybody was coming in this direction so that they could head out towards Khe Sanh to help with the

Lam Sam invasion out there, going into Laos. And the kids? The kids didn't know where they were going. We'd go, "Where are you going?" "I don't know." "When are you coming back?" "I don't know." They had no clue where they were going and they were petrified because they had no idea what was up or what they were going to do or when they'd be back. Nobody knew anything.

If you look up you saw helicopters in line, maybe fourteen, fifteen in a row. It was so crowded in Quang Tri that Chinooks were having to land in our backyard and the power of the Chinooks would move our little hooch. They were so powerful that they would blow our house. We would go out to Khe Sanh and the guys were too busy to do the fun and games, but we would talk to them. We would haul sand bags just to be there with them while they filled the sand bags with the red clay I hated so much. We were there just to talk to them, and just to let them know that we cared, but they had no idea what they were doing. We had no idea what was going on at that point in time. Nobody knew what was going on. They held our mail—they wouldn't let our mail go out, they didn't bring mail in. Now talk about a depressing thing for a vet: it is not to be able to receive mail and not even know why you're not getting your mail. And it was monsoon part of the time. It was just a really bad time.

The biggest part of it was we ended up having to spend the night out there. They couldn't come back and get us, so here they are trying to figure out what to do with two girls. How do we keep these girls safe out here? So they finally found an old jeep, an ambulance type of thing, and they let us spend the night in the ambulance. Well, here are two girls, locked in for our "own protection." They locked us in this old ambulance and they gave us a pot in case we had to go to the bathroom. They started having incoming and we could hear the incoming and they forgot we were there. We were going, "Hello, help, we'd like out," and meanwhile the incoming was coming in and we were locked in this ambulance.

I remember once we had to cook our dinner. It was a blackout condition, and we were all in this big tent and it happened to have some straw on the ground. It was the only place in the country I saw straw, and we were cooking our C-rations. You use a little bit of the C4 and you light it and it kind of like explodes a little bit before it burns. You could hold your C-rations over it and cook them, and I caught the straw on fire. Here the straw is starting to burn and all they could say was, "It's blackout conditions, it's blackout conditions," and we finally got the fire out.

By that time I was so numb that things weren't terrible. You could just be embarrassed that you caught the straw on fire or you could just be kind of upset that you couldn't have any sort of a shower or any sort of wash. The clay in Khe Sanh was just incredible. It was red, thick, heavy, dusty, clay. In fact, when we went by jeep we used to have to wear a bandanna because you couldn't breath it was so thick and so heavy and to have to keep that clay and that dust on you, was grimy, grimy.

We women did what we could do. For the war, basically, there were nurses. I couldn't be a nurse, and I did what I could do. I was there, I was willing to do what I needed to do, and that I would like to think that the sacrifice that the girls made was enough to warrant our name on the Wall. And to warrant veteran status even if I want to go have a drink at the American Legion. I've been offered membership in the Women's Auxiliary. I won't even have a flag on my casket when I die. But I think the biggest thing is, I was exposed to Agent Orange and I do have things that I would like to discuss with the doctors. If you tell your HMO that you have war-related injuries, there's a fine clause in your little fine print that says war-related injuries are exempt. And if you want to go to the doctors that know about Agent Orange, you have to be military.

I think we made life a little more bearable for the guys, at least that's what I'm hearing. I just got on the Internet and I'm hearing from guys from all over the United States, and that's what they're saying. They're saying, "You made us feel like it was worthwhile. You made us feel like it was worth getting up in the morning. You gave us a taste of home. You let us know that somebody cared, and that not all Americans were against this," that there were some people there supporting them.

I felt for so many years I had been living on the edge vacillating between a relatively normal life and then being depressed because of the things that had happened in Vietnam. I just knew I needed to get over it, and I wasn't doing it. Now I went back to Vietnam in 1998. It was my fiftieth birthday present to me from me. It was really the hardest thing I've ever done in my life. When I went to Vietnam the first time, I didn't know any better. When I went to Vietnam the second time, I knew that it was going to be life-altering. I was either going to come back with some closure, or I was going to come back completely crazy. It was going to alter my life somehow. I really do think it helped, I think it gave closure. I think it gave a sense of healing. I think it gave me a new Vietnam to think of. It's never going to erase the nightmares or the pain or some of the things that happened, but at least now I can have other memories, too, of Vietnam.

Everybody has flashbacks and nightmares and it could be this person's death or that person's death or stumps in the hospital walking. We used to go write letters for guys in the hospital, and I know that it was one of the hardest things to do because when guys lost an arm or a leg in Vietnam, they didn't close the wound. They kept it open because, from what I was told, conditions in the room were not sterile enough, so if they closed the wound, they would possibly get gangrene and have more surgery done. So they would keep it open until they could get them to Japan. Sitting there writing letters home for amputees and having to help guys go home on emergency leaves was part of our job too. The Red Cross would, if there was an emergency stateside, help arrange emergency leave for them. The fear, the incoming, the tear gas, the bad conditions, the people being killed all around us, the drugs, the alcohol, everything that we were exposed to all day, every day.

I remember that two things helped me most about the trip back. When I first got there I went back to Cu Chi where Ginny was murdered and I held a memorial service for her there, and that helped with closure. We went on up to An Khe, and I remember standing in front of what had been my first assignment, and the building wasn't there. Needless to say all the buildings are gone, and they had replanted the mountain and the trees were twenty-five years tall and whatever, and I kept looking at it, going, "This is not the way I remember this mountain. This doesn't look the way I remember the mountain at all," and I kept thinking, "If the earth is healed, I should."

Until I landed in San Francisco after my one-year tour, and it was one year—we promised a year—out of the twenty-six of us that went over in my class, six stayed the year. At the end of the year I was unemployed and in San Francisco.

You survived. You laughed a lot, you did not pay too much attention, and also I remember thinking that I was invincible. I remember by the end of my tour, I wouldn't even get up when the rockets were coming in. I had survived so much, that a rocket wasn't going to get me. I wouldn't even bother to get up and go to the bunkers. It was, "They missed, missed again," type of thing, because we had survived so much.

Born in Virginia in 1948, Susan Bradshaw McLean grew up in Virginia and North Carolina. She graduated from high school in 1966, where she had been a cheerleader and a class officer. At Longwood College in Virginia she majored in elementary education. Her goal was to teach but she joined the Red Cross and went to Vietnam. In 1971, after finishing her tour in Qui Nhon, she returned home to marriage, two children, and a career in teaching. In 1990, she "came out of the vet closet and went to

my first Vietnam veterans reunion." Reunions and the veteran experience have been part of her life ever since. That experience and Desert Storm made her realize she had "full-blown PTSD." She went in for treatment, eventually divorced, and moved from Hawaii to Florida where she now lives. In 1998, she finally returned to Vietnam and there she found closure. At Khe Sanh she uncovered pieces of sandbags she possibly helped fill with the hated red clay that penetrated everything it touched. She put samples of the volcanic red clay in Ziploc bags along with pieces of the sandbags and brought them home as tangible souvenirs of the war. Possessing her Master's degree in special education, she currently teaches teenage boys convicted of sexual felonies. In her classes she talks about Vietnam, "because we owe it to the students. Someone has to pass along what happened in Vietnam." This is important, she says, "In spite of civilian women getting no recognition for their role in Vietnam, for receiving no medical benefits and for not even getting a flag to cover our coffin when we die."

EMILY STRANGE
RED CROSS DONUT DOLLY

Emily Strange was in college during the Tet Offensive in 1968 and like many students had been an anti-war protester. She majored in English and graduated with a BS in Education but decided in 1969 to see the war for herself. She volunteered for the Red Cross and became a Donut Dolly and says, "Since we were not military, we had no rank." Soon after arriving in Vietnam, she realized her mother might have been right and she questioned why she was there. Her first assignment was in a Red Cross Mobile Unit from which she traveled around the country to visit forward area fire bases. Her permanent base was a dusty man-made port in the Mekong Delta, called Dong Tam, southwest of Saigon, home to the U.S. Navy's Riverine Force. In Vietnamese *Dong Tam* means "united hearts and minds."

I graduated from college and I had a degree in English education, and thought, "Gee, I just don't want to go back into the classroom. What else is available?" I just started going around looking and I went to the Red Cross and they said, "Well, we could send you to Vietnam or Korea." That sounded pretty exciting, and I thought, "If you're going to go you might as well go all the way." I knew people were killing and dying over there, and I didn't perceive that as a good thing. I perceived that there must be some better way to settle it.

Of course the war was on the news every night. You couldn't escape it. It hadn't occurred to me to go, but I had been a war protester and that was easy to be. It was very easy in my naiveté to believe that the war was wrong, to believe there's no reason to be killing and dying. Probably one of the greatest speakers I've heard at a Vietnam war rally was a general who had been there, and was against the war. I thought, he's been there, he knows what's going on, and if he's protesting, that means a lot more than war protesting is fun. Protesting was easy to do. There were a lot of fun people and partying and protesting, but I thought, the general has been there, he knows, he understands. I guess when the Red Cross said I could go, I wanted the opportunity to experience it, to know both sides, not just be the easy part here at home. I wanted to know the reality. Vietnam sounded so exciting, and because I had been protesting it, I wanted to know what was going on.

I think youth believes it will not die. It's one of those fallacies of youth. Though I had seen people dying in Vietnam on the TV, and I certainly saw people who were killed, it just really didn't cross my mind that I could die.

We actually had two weeks training in Washington, D.C. They told us we should always be lady-like, but I don't remember all of the training. The image of the nice girl back home is how you pictured the girl next door and that's sort of what we were supposed to be. Together with our class from D.C., the

Red Cross sent us to Vietnam. They flew us to San Francisco. We left from San Francisco, and we went through Alaska and Japan. Well, you had to fly over to Vietnam in—I guess they called them Class As. They were like nicer uniforms and high heels and, like a London Fog type of raincoat thing. That's what they told me to wear, so apparently what else should I be wearing? That's the only time I ever remember wearing them, though. Then we had little dresses or culottes, and I preferred the culottes because getting on and off of helicopters it seemed to me better to have on culottes, so I generally wore the culottes. When we arrived, the initial reaction when you walked off the plane was the heat and humidity and smell. It just took your breath away. It absolutely took your breath away. It was sort of a gasp. We landed at night. They got us off the plane and they took and put us on buses and the first thing we all noticed was that they had wire mesh over the bus windows. I don't know, I guess in your mind I sort of thought, "Well, gee, if this was a safe place, what's the mesh for?" I think we were all pretty stunned. Yes. Probably we were pretty stunned.

Then we had maybe a week in Saigon for sort of orientation. We were all headed to be Donut Dollies. I guess the next day in Saigon when you saw everybody carrying rifles, you realized you were in a big city, but everybody has guns. It made you question whether there was danger. It never occurred to me I would be in danger. There would be mortar attacks and they were pretty dangerous.

The last day in Saigon they put up the assignments as to where each of us was assigned. There was a list on the wall and your name and the place where you would be sent. Everybody looked and looked, and then they had a big map and then they'd go like, "Cu Chi," and they'd look on the map and go, "Oh, there it is, oh, Danang, there it is." I went, "Dong Tam," and I looked down that map and I looked up that map. . . . It wasn't even on the map. I'm thinking, "Where are they sending me?" So, then we all sat down and they sort of briefed us. They were saying things like, "You'll be living in a villa in the little town, and oh, they have beach there," and, I mean things were sounding really good, but they hadn't gotten to Dong Tam. They kept waiting, and when they finally got to it, they sort of saved that 'til last. They were actually sending two of us down there. A friend of mine went with me, and they said, "You're going to Dong Tam and it's down south. You'll be living on the main base camp, in a hooch, and they have either a lot of dust or mud, depending on the season and they get mortared. Okay," they said, "now let's all get ready." There were six Donut Dollies and we shared our hooch with special services. There were three of those hooches.

We ended up with a helicopter because we were not very far south of Saigon. I think some of the other women took planes, but they put us on a helicopter which is a unique experience the first time you do it. I kept thinking as they banked that my guitar was going to fall out.

Well, when we flew in to Dong Tam, it was the dry season and as you're landing, it was just like barren. It was like, "Well, am I landing on the moon or what?" It was really barren, and it was really hot, and somebody in a jeep picked us up and drove us to the hooch. I was there to keep up the morale of the troops. We created games like *Jeopardy* and *Wheel of Fortune* so you could divide the guys into two teams and we would use subjects like sports, music, movies, TV, anything that reminded them of home. It took them back to a time before there was the killing and dying, and for a few minutes they could be home. We also had a sister chapter that sent us things. They sent us cigarettes and Monopoly boards, and a lot of cards. Once they sent us bongo drums, and we would just carry them out to the field and give them to the guys because they had no PX out there. Whatever we could take them was like wonderful.

The Red Cross had several different programs in Vietnam. They had the hospitals, they had the service where when a relative died they got them home, and then they had, they called it Supplemental Recreation Overseas, and that's what I was, commonly known as Donut Dolly. The Donut Dollies were two types of units. One would be a club in the division base and the guys would come in from the field and be able to go to the club. Then we had the mobile units which is where I was, and I would get up in the morning and go down to the helicopter pad and get on a helicopter and fly to one of the fire bases. We'd carry our little game bag with us. Then they would set us down at the fire base and we would go from company to company, and a lot of times we played games. We'd divide the guys up and there was some fierce competition in those games. Sometimes there would just be a few guys and we would just sit and talk with them. I carried my guitar, and some places we'd just sit and sing. We would just improvise. If you got there and one of the units was fixing to go out, you would just go to them first and stand around and just talk with them. Maybe you would go down and wait at the field where the choppers were coming in, and just see them off. It depended on the circumstances the men were in as to what we actually did. I mean, it was a constant transition of going out and coming in. If they were coming in we would meet them at the choppers.

Sometimes they just wanted to be left alone and I could respect that. There was nothing on their mind but survival and when will it be my turn? And not thinking about those that had friends that were gone. It was an awful thing to see.

They always had smiles for us when we showed up. And

there was this thousand-yard stare that just looked right through you, and sort of focused on your face, and there was real confusion. It was contradictory to everything in his mind that there should be standing there an American woman looking at him. He looked real bewildered for a while and then he just broke out in this big grin. When they're getting ready to go out, you have to understand there is fear, though it's never spoken. You understand they're getting ready emotionally, not just gear-wise, but emotionally, to go out, so we just kept it light. And they always had smiles for us. I always put on that smile for them. You just always assume this was going to be fun and you were there to build morale and you had your smile on and you were just ready for whoever and whatever. That was your job. It didn't matter what had gone on with you, or that what had gone on with them was worse. It was your job to keep up their morale. You put on the smile anyway. So sometimes I called it my Eleanor Rigby face that I kept in a jar by the door. You got up, you put on your makeup and your Eleanor Rigby face and you went out. If the Donut Dollies were there, then it must be safe.

At Dong Tam it was like living in a goldfish bowl. It certainly was. There were six women, six Donut Dollies, and three special services, and there were like six thousand guys. The friend that went down with me said, "It's like going from a wall flower to a sex symbol just by crossing a tiny ocean." Sometimes there were times you just wanted to be left alone. I know for myself, we could go eat at the officers' mess, but I never went. Mostly I would eat my LRRP [Long Range Reconnaissance Patrol] rations alone. It was like freeze-dried food and I would eat that in the hooch, because I just wanted to eat. I didn't want to have to smile at anybody. I didn't want to have to talk to anybody. I didn't want to have to listen to anybody. I just wanted to eat dinner.

When we got in from the field, there were always parties. They would bring the men in to Dong Tam for what they call stand-down. It means you can go into Dong Tam and get drunk and party, and get away from the war for a few days. So when we got home from the day in the field, we would then look at the list of parties for that night, and you always felt like you wanted to at least make an appearance at them, particularly if it was guys that you really knew and really cared about. So, I just wanted to eat dinner in peace and then you would get ready and go out to the parties.

I'll never forget a young helicopter pilot named Kenny. If you give a nineteen-year-old kid a Corvette, they are so cool. They had given Kenny a Cobra helicopter with mini guns and rockets and everything. This was the ultimate. Kenny was wide-eyed and thrilled to death. There was so much of the child still left in Kenny. He was a good kid and when I came home from a run, they told me he was gone.

I mainly felt like I was there for the guys, and I would give as much as I possibly could, but there were some nights that I just didn't want to party and I just didn't go.

With all the horror of the Vietnam War and everything I experienced, I would still go to Vietnam again. It changed me forever and I gained strength from that time I would never have had, if I had not gone. I know there will be no mortars today. No one died today in the war. Looking back, that alone gives me strength. Today, what sometimes seems awful is, in the grand scheme of things, just a blip, and much easier for me to deal with. After returning from a recent reunion, the bond I have today with others who went through Vietnam is the strongest bond I have and that any of us has. I would gladly do it all over again if I had to.

KENNY

while i was out building morale
you
with your Cobra
were dying.

details are relative
your wife waits
unknowing that i think of her at this moment
or
that you never again will.

last night you were drunk
and we wanted to be alone
so we made excuses
and left you

i'm sorry now
but it's much too late for apologies
you're too busy derosing from the world
and being reassigned to eternity
to know how i feel.

dwelling upon the loss of a friend
is death in life

life is for the living
death is for the dead
and so Kenny,
we must now go our separate ways.

Emily Strange was born in Atlanta, Georgia. There, with her parents and one younger sister, she spent the first twenty-four years of her life. Her father was a warrant officer with the National Guard and her mother was a teacher. After attending Murphy High School in Atlanta, Emily went to Young Harris College in northern Georgia for two years. Then she transferred to Georgia Southern College, and graduated with a degree in English. Emily says, "College was just college and I majored in partying

and minored in English. It was the sixties, after all." After Vietnam, and a short spell in Atlanta, she moved to Florida. There she worked as a wood sculptor exhibiting year-round at outdoor art shows. Now she is an electronics engineer in Wisconsin with a Fortune 500 company where she works with and loves computers. As with many women who served in Vietnam, it took years for Emily to come to terms with her experience. "Putting pen to paper became the way I survived in Vietnam. I call it a gift from God." Emily had always put her poems in the drawer but she continued writing after coming home from Vietnam and continues to this day. "It is something I have to do to get Vietnam out of my system." It is more important to her that her poetry helps anyone who reads it. In 1992, one of her songs was sung on *Austin City Limits.* Although never interested in publishing her poetry, Emily has now put it on the Internet for all to read. Her main pastime is attending veterans' events. She goes to Washington, D.C., without fail, every Veterans Day.

ARMY WOMEN

MARILYN ROTH
WAC
(WOMEN'S ARMY CORPS)

Marilyn Roth joined the army in February, 1964. While at Fort Lewis, Washington, in 1967, a memo went out that there was a need in Vietnam for clerk typists, E-4 and above. They had to be volunteers and Marilyn had the desire and the right credentials. Roth says, "I thought this was exciting, so I signed to go." She had her orders by February, 1968. Her mom said, "You're going where?" Roth said it was too late for her to change her mind. She arrived in Vietnam in April of that year. Assigned to the WAC Detachment, Long Binh, a huge base outside Saigon, she was part of only the second group of army women to arrive in Vietnam. She first worked in G2, intelligence, as a specialist writing up encoded messages for helicopter pilots. Marilyn Roth then became a document controller in G3, training.

The enlisted women that were going to Vietnam volunteered. I said, "I'll go." And two months later I got my orders and I was on my way.

I just felt I wanted to see what it was like, and I just wanted to be adventurous. That's what part of being in the military is for, to volunteer to go places and see what everything is like and get a new experience. Which it was. My mother was not happy. She was really worried. She said, "No, you can't go." I said, "It's too late, I'm going already."

I was twenty-five, my mother lived in Miami. I had been in the army since 1964 and got out in 1967. Sixty days later I went back in. That's when I was in Fort Lewis and I decided to volunteer to go to Vietnam. I was twenty-five and basically the young ladies that were there were like between nineteen and twenty-three. So I was a little bit older and more mature and had more time in the military.

First of all, Jewish women don't join the army. But I came from Brooklyn and all my friends were on the wealthy side and I wasn't Jewish by richness. I was just Jewish and I couldn't afford to go to college or marry a doctor or a lawyer, so I decided to join the army. I felt I'd get to travel, I'd get an education, and get experience, which my friends back in New York have never experienced. I'm the one that's been all over the world, and it didn't cost me a penny. So being a Jewish girl in Vietnam was a rarity for six months, and then a friend of mine named Barbara Rubenstein, who I knew at Fort Lewis, came. So we were the only two Jewish women in Vietnam.

When I left for Saigon I was panicky. I was the only woman on the plane. I had all men on the plane. It was very, very hot, very. I was scared. I went to San Francisco, stayed there I think about two or three days and then got on the plane and eighteen hours later we arrived in Vietnam and it was monsoon. I had been on the plane for so long that when I got off I got caught in the rain because it was the first day of monsoon and I was soaking wet.

When we landed, all you heard was thousands of people screaming, and I couldn't imagine why. But I found out later that the plane that I landed on was the one that the boys were leaving to go home on. So they were cheering that their plane was on the ground and as soon as we got off and they filled up with fuel, they were getting on and going home.

I didn't know what they were doing, but I was so exhausted from the flight that I didn't care about anything else but getting to the barracks and meeting the CO and the first sergeant and finding my way around. They took me by bus to the orderly room. I arrived, and the first thing I did was say, "Can I take a shower?" And they gave me a white towel and a white washcloth and I took my stuff up to my room and took a shower. When I came back down, the towel and the washcloth were orange from the dust. Orange dust all the time, from the heat and the dirt and the mud, and the dust. It was awful. I said, "Can I call my cousin Danny?" who was stationed in Danang. They said, "Okay," so I picked up the phone and called him and I started crying. "Danny, can I please go home? I don't want to be here." He said, "But you just got here." After that I just realized that I had to stay.

We were fenced in outside Long Binh and then where we lived, we were fenced in and we had a guard at the gate. Women were secured. You had to have approval to go anywhere. If you went to work, they let you out, and when you came home from work they let you in and out, in and out. But by 10:30 every night you had to be in because we had bed check. So we were guarded twenty-four hours a day, inside and then outside. We went to work, we were guarded by the perimeter, and we had guards all over the place. And we had what we called the "reactionary force," which was a whole bunch of guys, infantry guys, who protected us all the time. That was their main job, not like the women in the Gulf where they had to go over with their weapons and they were required to protect themselves. If we ever needed full protection, then the men would be there doing that for us, and in case of emergency, we would be airlifted to Okinawa.

It wasn't jail, but it felt like it. The only time we were allowed out is if you had official business to go to, or if some boss of yours would say, "Let's go to Saigon for the day." He had to have a weapon, you had to go in a military vehicle, and you had to be protected by two men with two weapons, and you needed permission from the higher-ups in order to go. The only time I went out was to go to Saigon to get a passport to go on military leave for seven days and when I hopped a plane to go to Bangkok for R&R.

I felt protected, secure, and very special. I never felt that way since. I felt like I was really doing something important, and even though I spent almost twenty years in the military, I never felt that camaraderie and that closeness with anybody in my entire life.

I felt camaraderie with both women and men, and the Vietnamese themselves. They loved the Americans. I had red hair at the time and I had freckles, which is a rarity and the Vietnamese were always going like this to me, rubbing them, trying to take them off. They thought it was dirty, because they never saw anybody with freckles before. They called me Baby-san, and they used to say to me, "Baby-san, Baby-san, you take me to America I be free, I be free." Of course you couldn't take them, but they loved us, they loved us. They took very good care of us.

I worked in G2, which is intelligence, for six months. Then I worked in G3, which is training, for six months. I was a clerk typist and I typed up secret crypto messages to give to the helicopter pilots so that the helicopter pilots could communicate with the guys down on the ground. Lots of times, all the work that I did, if a helicopter got mortared, I would be noticed and I'd have to change all the codes again. It was very interesting. The secret crypto messages looked odd. That's all that I can remember. It was just different letters for different alphabets, for part of the alphabet, and every time something happened, the letters had to be changed. I used to type them up on this secret telegraph machine. I typed up each letter as a different symbol and that's how they would become a word. The keys would go to different symbols to make up ABCD and that's how they would communicate to the guys on the ground. The communication was where they were going to bomb next or where there was VC and so on. The messages were sent by chopper to the communications people, and that's how the guys on the ground would communicate with each other, by radio. It was very important work.

We couldn't screw up. No. Then after that, I went to G2 and I was in charge of two thousand secret documents, so if anybody came for messages I would log them in and log them out and I had to keep tight control about that. It was very intense.

They would kid around with me, saying that when I was going to reproduction section, I would have to go myself because there was nobody else in the office. So they put a pistol belt on me with a pistol and they said I had to wear it around my body so that I could grab it easily. I never fired a weapon before, and I really thought that they meant it, that I would really have to—in case anybody planned to attack me—wear it from building to building. These documents had to be protected. I was cracking up because the belt wouldn't fit me. I weighed

210 pounds, and they were saying that they'd have to go get an extension on the pistol belt so I could go out by myself. We were laughing. They were cracking up and I started laughing too when I realized it was a joke and that one of the men would escort me to the building, to the repro building.

The men were glad that we were there. All they saw were Vietnamese women, and they used to call the American women round-eyes. Especially on the posts where all the GIs were, we were treated with the utmost respect. Not one cuss word. We never heard anything derogatory about us. We were like brothers and sisters, and they treated us like we were angels, they were so glad that we were there. Even the outsiders, the NATO GIs, the Australian Army or the British Army that came in for certain kinds of training on the post treated us right. We'd meet them at the club at night and all they wanted to do was sit and talk to us, because they were out in the bush all the time, and they didn't see any American women. When they saw us they practically kissed our feet. We were like heaven-sent. No matter what you looked like, here I was 210 pounds, but I was an American woman, and they wanted to be with all the girls. It was unbelievable. We had a lot of fun.

I was there a week, only my first week, and I was at the club, and we were not allowed to wear pants. If you got our of your uniform, you wore a dress and stockings, and shoes, high heels or flats, whatever they were wearing those days. It was just part of being a woman in the army. Even on a post in the United States you dressed that way. Unless you were going to a sporting event, you were dressed as a lady, because in the early days in the sixties women wore dresses. We didn't wear pants. We wore our Class As in the United States and the only time you were allowed to wear pants was when you got to go off post to a sporting event, if you went bowling or you went to a ball game. But if you went out and you were going to a bar or you were going to a party, you had to wear a dress or a skirt. It was the military's way of saying, "You're women in the army, you're not boys, you're not men. We want you to dress like ladies." That's what we were called: ladies. We weren't called soldiers, we were called ladies and we were treated as ladies. You had to wear nail polish, you had to wear makeup, you had to wear lipstick, you had to be just perfect. We wore skirts all the time until 1976 when they came out with a pant suit, and that's when we kind of like went to fatigues.

Once I was at the club when all of a sudden we heard a siren sound. We did not know what it was. All the lights went out on the post because you can't have any lights on in case they're flying above and they could see us. So the lights went out, and they said, "Okay, everybody out of the club, get in back of the deuce and a half." I couldn't get up in the deuce and a half so I had to lift my dress up because all the girls were getting up into the back of the truck and they practically had to lift me up. Driving back to the barracks was traumatic because of the darkness. You couldn't even have the headlights on. After that I wasn't afraid anymore.

But the scariest part was on February 15, 1969, at two o'clock in the morning. We were all sleeping and we hear the alert and all the lights go out. And on top of my locker was my pistol belt and my canteen and my helmet. But also on top of the locker were my speakers to my Sony reel to reel. The first thing you have to do is grab your pistol belt. But I hadn't used it in a while so I just grabbed onto it, and as I grabbed onto it, it got entangled with the speaker, and the speaker came and fell on my head, and I thought that a mortar came through my room and hit me. Everybody is dragging me out of the room, and I'm screaming, "I've been hit, I've been hit." So they take me to the bunker and I'm sitting in the bunker and I'm hysterical: I've been hit, no blood anywhere, but I've been hit. My commanding officer comes around and hears me crying and says, "What's the matter with you?" I said, "I've been hit," but she knew that I wasn't hit, so she said, "You're an idiot." The next morning when we went back to our rooms we found out it was the speaker that had hit me on the head. I could not live that down to the day that I left in April.

There was incoming rocket fire, most of the time, throughout the year that I was there. The post office got mortared and destroyed. Our executive officer got killed. They found—the next morning—fifteen Viet Cong outside the perimeter, dead. The VC were told that if they could take over Long Binh, that Long Binh had a large supply of C-rations and that's food and that they will get C-rations. They already had the can openers in their possession, but they never took over. They were going to try to take over the post.

As an enlisted woman in Vietnam, very, very few people know, or understand what we were doing there. I have a license plate on my car that says "Served in Vietnam," and I get stopped lots of time at a red light when the windows are down and a guy would say, "Oh, where were you stationed? What hospital were you in? You were a nurse?" And I would say, "I was enlisted," and they wouldn't even talk to me. They would just take right off, because they don't care about us. Basically, they know nurses. They do know there were the nurses. They don't know much about us. As far as I know, the jobs that women did in Vietnam were mostly clerical. And that's about it; administration, communication, signal, but basically it was clerical. Support, yes.

Many a night when we thought we might have an alert we had to sleep in our fatigues because our commanding officer was very strict and she took very good care of us. She felt that the fatigues would protect us. There were about eighty of us, all in the clerical field, and we came from all over. As each woman left, another woman would come in to replace her. The year that I was there, a lot of women came and went, and there were always about eighty. We lived in old barracks and then they built new barracks for us, where we lived like five girls to a room in the barracks. If I remember, it was on two levels, and the senior NCOs [non-commissioned officers] had their own room. The commanding officer had a trailer.

We never really listened to what went on outside of Vietnam. We just cared about what was going on there every single day in our jobs and what we were going to do after work. We worked seven days a week, twelve hours a day . . . seven days a week, twelve hours a day. Then as soon as we got off work we'd go have something to eat and we'd go to the club and dance and have a nice time. They had Vietnamese bands who played American music—rock 'n' roll, country and western. We had drinks like they do in the United States, and we would sit there, drink and dance to the band, and have a party. Then we would come back to the barracks, go to sleep, wake up the next morning, and get ready to go to work. We had a couple of what were called enlisted clubs. We got bused to work every day to the headquarters building and we worked our twelve hours and every day we did the same thing, day after day after day.

The two girls that I remember most at the time were Pat Landry and Phyllis Williams. Pat Landry found me about three years ago. The *VVA* magazine did an article on me and they had a picture of myself and Pat Landry. We can't find Phyllis Williams yet. We don't know where she is. I took a picture of the three of us and sent it to the *VVA* magazine and Pat, we call her Priscilla now, her name is Priscilla Wilkowitz, but then she was Pat Landry. She married this guy Ken, who she met and dated in Vietnam and a year later they got married, and they have been married ever since. He remembered me, and he said, "Hey, Priscilla, look at this, there's Marilyn." So she wrote a letter to the *VVA* magazine, they wrote a letter to me, and I called her and we cried for an hour, after twenty-nine years. Then, we went to the Windsor Memorial in October a year ago, and at the reunion, at the armory in D.C. we found thirteen of us all together. It was so thrilling. It was like we had just seen each other the day before. They were still bossing me around— "Hurry up Marilyn," and "Hurry up Marilyn," and "Come on, let's go, Marilyn," the same way they treated me in Vietnam. It was the same way they treated me there. It was four days of nothing but just wonderful, wonderful.

If I had $4,000 to pay for the trip, I would like to go back to Vietnam, because I'd like to see what I left behind.

Marilyn Roth left the WACs in 1969 after returning from Vietnam. She then married and when her marriage ended in 1971, she re-enlisted. The army then became her career until in 1982 she had to retire for medical reasons. Her rank on retirement was an E-7, Sergeant First Class. Over the years, she has been a manicurist at Nail Tech, worked as a cashier at K-Mart, and is now learning the art of picture framing. She lives in Melbourne, Florida.

NANCY JURGEVICH
WAC
(WOMEN'S ARMY CORPS)

After a staff job and a Detachment
Command in the United States, Captain Nancy Jurgevich, a career officer in the Women's Army Corps, had
the distinction of being selected Detachment Commander in Vietnam.
She says, "It was an honor with a lot
of responsibility. It was the highlight of my career." She arrived in
South Vietnam in October, 1968, at Long Binh, where she was in
charge of a detachment of between sixty and one hundred women
who had administrative jobs in communications, logistics, intelligence, and engineering.

I did not have any fears before I arrived there, but reality did
set in after I was there a few days. I was a little bit shocked even
though the military had educated me very well. I then realized
that the safety, health, and welfare of sixty to one hundred
women depended on me twenty-four hours a day. Their safety

233

was my number-one responsibility. The members of the detachment were young, outstanding American women with little fear. The women were so dedicated to their profession, to their duties, and most of all to the United States of America at a time when many Americans were turning their back on the United States. They were a unique group of women from all walks of life and many different backgrounds and cultures who pulled together as a team and functioned very well. They knew they were the select few that got to go to Vietnam. The military selected the best women. Most of the enlisted women were barely out of their teens. They were put into an entirely different living and working environment. The demand was there for them to work seven days a week, twelve hours a day. They were so dedicated, that they loved their jobs, they loved their bosses, and they liked being there. They were tired. Everybody got tired. There's no question about that, but they hung in there and did it with pride. They were so professional. They were strong women.

The living conditions were not great. Most of the women had about ten square feet of living space. We usually had hot water for the showers. Their off-duty time, which was very little, was spent on the patio or at some of the clubs in Long Binh. They were required to be back at the WAC Detachment at 10:00 P.M. every night. Our patio was used for movies almost every night and to socialize. We were fortunate enough to have an above-ground swimming pool that was donated and shipped over to us by the WAC veterans in Miami, Florida. That was a big day because everything down in Long Binh was hot and sweaty and that pool was a big deal.

Probably my biggest problem was when we had alerts and keeping those women in the bunkers until the all-clear was given. The bunkers were not a fun place to be. We were crowded in there and not a bit comfortable, but they were the safest places to be. The women hated being in there and would think of any reason to get out of them, such as going to the bathroom, being thirsty, thinking they were sick.

A few stories about alerts and bunkers. Early one evening we got hit relatively early and the sirens went off. One woman was frying eggs in an electric skillet. Somebody else came with her paper plates and their plastic forks, and they were going to have their little picnic lunch in there. Instead of worrying about helmets and canteens, they were worried about bringing dishes and utensils to the bunkers. Boy, the first sergeant let them have it. But you have to look at this thing, hey, they've got to have some kind of an out. You have to keep encouraging them. You have to keep saying, "Look, the helmet is a little more important, right?" Some of them would drag tape recorders to the bunkers trying to tape the noise from the rockets coming in. They all wanted to be at the edge of the bunker rather than the center of the bunker. They could tape easier that way and they wanted ten people to be in the space for one. They would keep the tapes for history and for themselves. I'm sure there are some of those tapes floating around now.

I hated going through the barracks. That was their living quarters and they did not have a lot and I wanted to give them as much freedom and privacy as possible. The only time I would go into their quarters was when the first sergeant insisted, especially if it had something to do with their safety and well-being. One day I heard the first sergeant telling them that if they did not get their areas straightened up that night, she was going to have me go through their barracks and they knew I did not like to do that. Stereo equipment had become available in the Post Exchange and those women had enough wiring around in their confined areas to hang a number of people. That is what the first sergeant was concerned about. Well, sure enough, that night we had an alert and one of the women did not straighten out her area. When the sirens were going off, we heard this woman screaming, "I've been hit." She was hit on her head, but with her new stereo which was on top of her field gear, her helmet and canteen. After I told her that she was hit on her head with her new stereo, she was concerned about the stereo being broken. I just told her to get herself in that bunker and stay there. I did not want to hear anything else about the stereo. But she was very dedicated, and she always had a good sense of humor. She had an outstanding job performance and she was always very loyal and very honest.

Another time in the bunkers, one of the women wanted to get out and fill her canteen, so the first sergeant gave her her canteen and told her to drink the water from hers. After the woman drank the water, she complained that it was old. The stories of the bunkers could go on and believe you me, I hated those bunkers as much as the women did, but they were life-saving devices.

As the commander, I tried to break the routines of Long Binh and allow the women to do something different once in a while. We did two field trips worth noting. We had a helicopter company who invited us to come down to their unit for the day, a training day. The women had to volunteer to fly down to this unit to enjoy a helicopter ride, an in-ground pool, and a cookout. Of course, ninety-nine percent of the women volunteered to go on this field trip. This would be a real treat for my women. They flew the helicopters to Long Binh and picked us up. When we arrived at the unit, those guys really treated us well: very polite, nice pool, great food. It was phenomenal. I mean, they had everything. That was a big break for the women. It gave them something different. A nice day was had by all.

The other field trip was to Saigon. The Vietnam Women's Training Center commander invited us to come to Saigon and see their training center. Of course, ninety-nine percent of the women volunteered to go on this field trip, too. We took security guards on the bus with us to Saigon. We took a big chance going down dangerous Route 1 from Long Binh to Saigon. When we arrived at the training center, we were greeted by the director of the Vietnamese Women's Army Corps. The women were really impressed with her. She gave us a tour of the barracks, and showed us how the women lived. We mixed with some of the women who were in training there, we saw their eating facilities, and we were just welcomed with open arms. Originally I had told them we would go to a very nice restaurant in downtown Saigon. Well, it was a little difficult because the first-class restaurants were not going to take eighty-plus people. We had thought about staggering them out to different restaurants as we had counterparts down there who were American who could have gone with them. In the meantime, the director of the Vietnamese Women's Army Corps came up with the idea she would take us to a special place called Cheap Charlie's. We could not change that. We were her guests, so I said, "Oh, my word, how am I going to tell these women that they're not going to some fantastic restaurant?" The women were very accepting when I explained the situation. Cheap Charlie's was just a basic little restaurant. Well, they were very nice, but the name alone kind of portrays it. The owners did put some flowers on the table for the occasion and everyone had lunch at the same place. The American women were so intrigued with the Vietnamese women and our American

women advisors that the nature of the restaurant became sec-
ondary. They had a great time. So we didn't get to go to the ex-
clusive restaurants, but it shows the women were more
interested in hearing the stories and talking to the women in
Saigon. That afternoon we went to the Saigon Zoo. It was certainly a great break from Long Binh. After a few hours, we mo-
tored safely back to Long Binh.

Thirty years later I really like to think about those two field
trips. I guess that's what age does to one. Again, my time in
Vietnam was the highlight of my career. The line and staff
women were outstanding, dedicated and extremely motivated.
Every generation of military women contributes their share to
their country. I really believe that World War II women laid the
groundwork. They got it started and it was our job to carry on
and I certainly think the women who served in Vietnam con-
tributed their share. They volunteered to be in the military,
they wanted to be in whatever was going on, and most of them
look at the time they were in the military as a positive experience. I've talked to many women who say it was a very important time in their life, and they will always treasure that. You're
talking about youth. They knew they were part of history, but I
don't think it meant as much then as it does today to them. As
we've all grown a little older and matured, we've had time to
think about it.

We had our first Vietnam Women's Veteran's Conference
in Florida in 1999 and it has brought us back together as a
unique group of women that performed as a team during the
Vietnam conflict. The result of the conference renewed a bond-
ing that will not be broken.

Nancy Jurgevich was born in 1940 in Stoyswood, a small town with a population under four hundred in western Pennsylvania. She grew up in the shadow of the region's steel mills, where her father worked to support a family that included her two brothers and her mother, who took care of the home. After graduating Forbes High School, she says, "I went into the military right out of high school and enlisted in 1958. Because I came from a small town, there weren't too many options available at that time as far as what I wanted to do. I knew one thing, I

wanted to travel, I wanted to do something different than become a housewife or work in a factory because that's about all that they had to offer. I had always respected the military and always had a great feeling about seeing a person in a military uniform. I went down to Fort McClellan, Alabama, for basic training. It was a whole new exposure to my life. I was a cryptographer at one time and went in the Signal Corps. After several stateside assignments and two tours in Europe, I returned to Fort McClellan and I went to officer's candidate school." Being selected to a command position in Vietnam was an important honor for Captain Jurgevich. "It was where all the action was at the time. I felt that's what we had been in the military for, and that's what we trained for. I was very pleased that I was selected because that was a position that was the envy of a lot of people. I was very proud." After leaving Vietnam in December, 1970, she returned to Fort McClellan, Alabama. While in the army she earned her BA from George Washington University and her Master's from the University of Utah. After Vietnam she had assignments at Command Headquarters in Atlanta and Command Headquarters Europe, based in Germany. She served in the Pentagon before retiring as a Lt. Colonel in 1984 after twenty-six years in the army. Jurgevich has the Legion of Merit and the Bronze Star with two Oak Leaf Clusters.

In her retirement, Nancy Jurgevich continues her dream of traveling and journeys to places as varied as the Yucatan Peninsula and a barge trip through France. She walks as much as she can and playing golf is her passion.

DORIS "LUCKI" ALLEN
WAC
(WOMEN'S ARMY CORPS)

After seventeen years in the WACs, army veteran Doris "Lucki" Allen finally went to South Vietnam in October, 1967. She says she was old when she was there in Vietnam, older than most of the troops and even her officers. At the sprawling Long Binh base and headquarters outside Saigon, her first assignment was to interrogate prisoners of war. That proved fruitless and she became an intelligence analyst working with captured documents, bomb damage assessments, after-action reports, and her own network of sources. Allen ended her tour of duty in Saigon working with enemy documents, learning from them, to her shock, that the North Vietnamese had put a price on her head. She returned to the United States in September, 1970 after three years in Vietnam.

My brother had come home from World War II, and we were all sitting there at home. My brother and sister were sitting

241

there just laughing, and I could see his heart. He had on a T-shirt, and I could absolutely see his heart pump through his shirt. I was like fourteen or something, fifteen whatever, but I saw his heart and I asked him what happened, and he told me. The poor boy was actually shell shocked, but it came out a lot of ways and I said I'm going to get them for that, and so in the back of my mind somewhere, I had put all that stuff.

I taught school when I finished college. My principal told my students that they could chew gum. He brought the Beech-Nut gum man in and said, "Here he is," and introduced him and I said, "Remember students, you can't chew gum in my class." They said, "Yes, Miss Allen." He said, "It's all right if they chew gum." "No, they can't, Mr. Dragel, no gum chewing," I said. "Yes, Ms. Allen," he said, "You can chew gum today, students." I tendered my resignation and I walked out. I did some substitute teaching for my sister, and then I said, "Geez, I'm going military," so I went in the military. The Korean War was on and I said, "I'm going." Somewhere it was there in the back of my brain. I still don't know the reason, but hey, why not? I'm sure I patterned my desire for the military after my brother and though I was a college graduate, I wanted to go through the ranks. The army was a wonderful learning place for me.

I first arrived in country at Tan Son Nhut Air Base. I guess there were two hundred-and-something men on the plane, and me. When everybody got there, all the men had their assignments and the trucks come to pick up the men. They were told they were assigned to such-and-such place and unit, and I was just standing there. I had on my class A uniform, thought I was looking cute, you know, sharp. I'm the only person dressed like this, and here I am in Vietnam, a combat zone, geez. People are snapping pictures. I went over and stood at the wall of the building in the airport, and I kept turning, and hiding my face because that was strictly paranoia. I didn't want them to take my picture, because I didn't know what I was doing. I kept saying, "Where am I going?" They kept saying, "Well, we don't have any place for you to go. We don't have any orders." I said, "Here are my orders." They didn't have anything to do, so they eventually took me down to the 90th Replacement. One of the first things that happened, my biggest memory, they gave me a white towel and a white washcloth. I had been there quite a few hours. I went in and took a shower, and I'm standing there, and I looked at my white wash cloth, and all I could think of is, "Oh my God, I'm turning white!" All of that was the red clay and the dirt of Vietnam. That was my very first thought. "God, I'm turning white," because it all came off.

At Long Binh, one particular day the officers come into the army operations center to get intelligence reports, and I'm the only intelligence sergeant sitting there. There's nobody else. So they have to come to me. I'd say, "Okay, don't take this convoy up to Song Be because it's going to be ambushed." They walk on out, and take the convoy up there anyway, and it was hit. In this one case, five ammo flatbeds just were gone. Five GIs, never to be back again. They're dead. I think it was nineteen wounded. They didn't have to do that. It made me feel ignored. But, I said, I have to keep going, because it's my job, and if they don't listen, it wasn't that I didn't give them the information. All the reports came over my desk and when you see it come back, you know exactly what happened. So, had they listened it would not have happened. When I'm trying to give them information, they still need to read a piece of my heart.

There were several other things that were hard. They'd walk in and ask for a bomb damage report, bomb damage, BDA. I'd say, "Oh, it was such-and-such on such-and-such a hill"—because my contacts had already given me the information. So the officer comes in, and says, "But what do you have to say about that?" "I already told you where it was." "I want that information on my desk." But I already did that, okay. So the kick is, you either get bitter, or you just go on and say, forget it, keep doing your work, and that's what I did. I kept doing my work.

What they did made me feel ignored. Being black. Being a woman. Being a WAC. Being in intelligence. Black. Woman. Very tough. And at the time I was a specialist. These prejudices, I know they're going around in my brain, black, woman—got no business here. WAC, you're not supposed to be in the army—this is a man's job. Intelligence, ah, oxymoron. Specialist. You're a specialist, you're not a sergeant, you're not a master sergeant, you're not an NCO, but that's what I was. I was all those things. They would look at me and try not to show disdain for who I was. But I could tell how they felt. I could see it in their eyes. Where did you come from and what is going on here? This is not by the "book." So you respond the best way you can. When I got to be a warrant officer it was a bit different, but just a tick, really very little.

I was an intelligence analyst. At first I was an interrogator of prisoners of war. That's what I went over as, and then they found out that it was not really expeditious to go out to the field and do the interrogations. I did a couple in my detachment when I first got there. I would ask the captured soldiers where they came from and where they were going. I didn't need to know their name, rank, and serial number. My superiors wanted that information but I didn't care. Their name and rank meant nothing. I wanted to know if they were pointing rockets at us. But the officers decided those interrogations were not expeditious, so I moved into being an intelligence analyst. I worked myself into being in intelligence, period. All these reports come on to my desk every day, and I had bundles of them. I put them on the side of the desk, and then I'd look through them. I'd throw some out and put the others in a pile that I thought maybe somehow would come together.

The reports came in from all over Vietnam. They came from every single combat unit in Vietnam—every single one. I got reports on everything that they did. Everything was written down on paper, okay. Reports came in when you shoot at someone, and when someone got shot. I had all KIA [killed in action] reports, all WIA [wounded in action] reports. All of those. Everything. Then I had reports how the battle took place, because it was a catalog of events. Whether it was a lie or not, I got it. I had my own sources all over the country. I had a field telephone beneath my desk against regulations. Often I got reports direct from the field. The officers would look at me with anger and awe when I used it but they did nothing about it. My information was firsthand. My job was to give them the truth the way I saw it on the ground but by the time it got to the Pentagon, it was often skewed.

I had this power, okay, but I also had power in these piles of documents. In these piles I also had information that they had gotten from the "woodsmen," South Vietnamese who collected firewood in the jungle and reported what they saw. Sometimes we had information from those paid informers, or people that just wanted to talk. People in the field wrote everything down, so all those reports came in as information, and then I'd pick them up and I'd go through them. The next day, another pile would come in. What I would do is, I'd take this pile at the end of the day and go through it. Some I threw out, but it's all in my brain by then, so I threw some others out. I got there toward the end of October. Two months prior to my going to Vietnam I knew I was going. I said, "Geez, I'm going to clean up my mind, so when I get there, I'll have a really clean slate from which to work." That was okay, but when I got on the plane, all I did was sit there and I read the newspapers. I knew the entire order of battle, that is to say I knew every place that Americans were. I knew where our allies were. I knew how many troops were there, I knew everything, just because it was in the newspaper. The media reported it. So everybody knows it because you could read the newspaper. You know where all our troops are, and what they're doing. At any rate, I had cleaned my mind. I was ready.

While I was there we had a couple rounds hit like close to the compound. The largest ammo dump in the world at that time got hit and it went up. I'm standing in my room looking out, and I say, "Wow." I stood at the door, and I'm looking at it all go up, and I got knocked back in my room, under my bed, by the shock wave. I said, "Oh my God, I'll never look at that again." But we did.

My job, as opposed to synthesize, was to turn information into intelligence that we could use offensively or defensively. In December, 1967, I wrote a report, and what it said is, that geez, fifty thousand Chinese are going to come over here and clobber the bejezus out of us. One of the reasons I called them Chinese is because I hadn't been there long enough to really know where all these people come from. Everything I looked at said all these Viet Cong were dead. There were none left. We killed them all. So where is the enemy coming from? North Vietnam was on my brain, so I said they were fifty thousand Chinese. The Viet Cong had been wiped out. The enemy got to come from somewhere and I said fifty thousand Chinese. I took it into my G2 and he says, "Nah," but I convinced him to please let's do something about it. He let me take it up to MACV [Military Assistance Command Vietnam] headquarters. When I got to MACV headquarters I handed it to the guy at the sergeant's desk, and he went all the way through his chain of command. It must have taken an hour and he came back out and said, "Nah, I don't think we better do this, we better not do this." I just died inside. "What do you mean you can't do this? You've got to do this. They're coming, they're going to do it, and they're going to do it at such-and-such a date." I did not have the day. I had no idea what Tet was. All I knew was that in this time frame, this is what's going to happen. If we don't do something about it, we're going to be clobbered. So, Tet was actual. You've read about and heard about the Tet Offensive. One of the reasons that I still cry, I'm full of rage in one sense, but I'm not angry, but I think that maybe two thousand of those men out on the Wall belong to me, and the reason I say that is I think had they listened, maybe all those people wouldn't have been dead. Don't get me wrong, I don't feel guilty. I mean, there's no guilt for it, there's no concern because I can't do anything about it. I have PTSD, and I think it helps it stay with me. The feeling is still there, though. You can't just take something out and say it doesn't exist. It does exist, it's still there. I can't talk about the government because they're just people too, but those people will never be accountable, okay. I'm not bitter. I'm not angry with anybody.

I carried a weapon because I was allowed. I went to Saigon a lot and it didn't make sense to get caught with no help for the job I did. So I just had to have help. I never fired it. But I sure felt better carrying it if I'd have to do a courier run or just run up to Saigon. There was always a chance of ambush, even though the roads were really protected. But there was always a chance, always a danger. I did not experience incoming hitting my immediate place. Five of my friends went to kingdom come. We had just left the Quonset hut between three and five minutes earlier, and they were in the ordnance outfit. A friend of mine and I just left, gone back to the hooch, and one 22mm rocket came in and blew them to bits. So, there you are.

One day I heard my name was on an enemy document. I just heard it, I didn't see it. My first thought was, "Hey, I'm important here." I had no idea how they got my name. The second time I saw my name on an enemy document it said that I was to be eliminated. I said, "Hmm, hmm, okay," but no problem. I did my work. We had captured a whole slew of documents along the Ho Chi Minh Trail when we hit a VC hospital, called Hospital 200. The truck also picked up documents from Laos and Cambodia. It was just full, full. They'd bring in truckloads, and I, at the time, was in charge of the translation branch. All the documents that were captured anywhere were brought into the documents exploitation center, and we had whole skids of people translating documents. A lot was just stuff, but a lot of them were real stuff. Then I saw it on one of those batches of documents that came off that truck. One of the workers back there saw my name and ran up and gave it to the Vietnamese guy in charge, and she kept looking at me and was excited and I said, "Okay, what's up?" I walked over and he said, "Well..." and I looked and I said, "Oh my God." That's when I saw it, my name. I kind of wished I kept one... no, I don't wish I'd kept one of those documents, because I didn't even like taking pictures. I said, "I've got to go home." I said to myself, "Okay, I've got to go home now. Don't try to stay. God gave you a couple of chances, just go home." I most certainly did. I most certainly did. I put in my papers. The VC got my name somehow. The Vietnamese people were not stupid. It doesn't surprise me that they were so resourceful in their own country. Maybe it was a Cheu Hoi, a defector. One former major in the North Vietnamese Army worked for me, going around the country training our troops how to spot and handle enemy sappers. Maybe him. I don't know. So I started carrying a weapon to protect myself.

I was in Saigon for six months, and experienced some stuff. I worked at Tan Son Nhut at MACV, five blocks from where I lived. I walked from my house to my office—five blocks with nothing in-between. We were in bunkers all the time at Tan Son Nhut, and, of course I feared for my life. I was living in a hotel and I would walk to work every day with all the "cowboys," the wild Vietnamese kids, and just plain people. I carried that .45 on me. One day a guy came along and grabbed my briefcase . . . grabbed it. I held onto it, and that's when I learned how to cock my .45 when it was behind my back, and I'd really like hold it down. I thank God I never had to use it. Would I have? This is just not reflection. I most certainly would have. I might have regretted it the rest of my life. Then again, maybe not.

From the time I walked into Vietnam to the time I left, I feel I did more good than harm, number one. I think I helped save lots of lives, number two. In fact I joked after I left country and we would talk about it. I said, I fixed it up for them, they can do the rest now, but I left them in good hands. But at no time, at no time, did I ever feel that it wasn't mine to do. I never looked for any and I never thought there was an end to any tunnel. I never thought there would be an end to the war. I never thought about that song that says, "One day at a time, sweet Jesus," you're here to do a job. Do your job, I thought, and when you're through with it, you're through with it. I haven't been able to get it out of me. My PTSD did not get me until the Gulf War. There was all of that long time in between Vietnam and the Gulf. One of the things, when President Bush said, "Okay, Saddam Hussein is going to put a lot of stuff out, some mustard gas and all that. I want you to dig a little foxhole and take your shelter hat, take your mask with you, your protective mask and I want you to put that over your head and crouch down so none of it will get on you." Whew! Do you realize how helpless they were? Absolute helplessness. They were absolutely helpless. Because we were sitting in Vietnam, we didn't know how helpless we really were. We didn't realize the man said, "Okay, if somebody shoots at you, don't shoot back"—not in those same terms exactly. There's only so much you can do—we can't attack that, we can't do this, we can't. . . . And it was the same thing of helplessness that those Gulf troops out there had, and so it all came in just a big wave. The Gulf War was the trigger. The Gulf War had nothing to do with me, but it had everything to do with me, because we were in that same situation. It was a matter of, they were over there and people said "welcome home" when they got back, and a lot of Vietnam veterans said, "Hell, all they did when we got home was leave us with a half-built ship." So that caused stuff for a lot of them. I'm a Ph.D. in psychology and I don't always think that way. I was in my 40s when I got to Vietnam. I was mature when I got there so I was a little different.

I'm proud of my life, but what does pride do? There's a song that says, "I've had my fun if I don't get well no more." I think I've lived my life from the time I was a tot, and everything else I can remember. I think I have absolutely lived this life, and I think I've lived it well. I have no regrets. Not long ago I had an accident and I thought I was going to die because I heard this voice say, "She's going down." I thought they meant me. I thought they meant me and I accepted it. I said, "please," and I wrote a note to get my family, because they were going to let me die. They got my family, but before my family got there, in the meanwhile, I don't know how long it was, every drop of pain, and I was in pain so bad you couldn't touch me, you couldn't touch my skin, I would almost scream, but between the time they got there when I knew I was going to die, every drop of pain, every drop went away. I didn't have any pain. It was just like I was ready to go, so I'm ready now. I'm ready to go. My sister came in, bless her heart, and she told me, "Baby, you're not going to die." "What's all this?" I said, I wrote and told her what happened. She said, "Oh no, baby, you're not going die, they weren't talking about you." I guess, I don't know how many minutes it was, but all my pain came back, every drop of it. So that's how I know that everything's fine with my life, with all of me. I think I've done well and I can go at any moment.

Vietnam taught me that I could drink like a fish every day, and I didn't have to be an alcoholic. I'm not trying to be funny, but it taught me—let's don't say it taught me, let's say, thank God for the experience. I was in the military. Military people go to war. I think I was very fortunate to have been allowed to go to war because many people volunteered and couldn't go, especially women. Vietnam was working every day and that's all that was. It's just the job. Sometimes I'd work twenty-two hours a day. I'd go home and get two hours of sleep and go back and work again. The adrenaline was so up, it wasn't a matter of we're at war, it was a matter of do your job. Like I said, when they didn't take advantage of my knowing, my expertise, my brilliance, if you will, not being funny, and you don't take advantage of it, I think that's dumb. So I had to figure, that's your loss, but do I dwell on that or do I go on at work? Vietnam to me was, yes, an experience. The camaraderie I wouldn't give up for anything in world. I wouldn't give up anything. I'm glad I went. I take Vietnam seriously right at this moment. I have no regrets. Do I think Vietnam was right? No. My biggest question, but not only for Vietnam's sake, is I still want to know, why do people kill people?—to show people that killing people is wrong.

Doris "Lucki" Allen was born and grew up in El Paso, Texas. Lucki says, "My mother was a cook in 'rich folks' homes,'" because she cooked for white families. My father, a barber 'downtown,' cut white folks' hair." Lucki has always been involved with music, and recalls that her school had a "little band that played in the first Sun Bowl parade." She fondly remembers the band wearing purple skirts and white capes and they

looked good marching. After graduating high school, she attended Tuskegee Institute in Alabama where she earned her degree in physical education. Because she believed in Booker T. Washington's decree of giving back to the community, she went to work as a teacher at Greenwood High School in Greenwood, Mississippi. She playing trumpet, and her sister, working nearby, formed a jazz combo and they played gigs all over the state. While they were playing, whenever her sister had a piece of bad luck, Doris had good luck. So she picked up the nickname Lucki, and it continues to this day. Influenced by her brother's experience in World War II, Lucki, tired of the private sector, joined the WACs in 1950 and decided to make the army her career. She returned from Vietnam in late 1970 and received her Master's degree while based in Germany. She resigned from the army as a Chief Warrant Officer 3 in 1980, after twenty-nine years, six months, and twenty-nine days, or officially thirty years and retirement. She earned her Ph.D. in psychology but had to slow down after a serious accident in 1986. Once an avid golfer, she says she is "still avid, just not a golfer." She became active in her church and spends much of her time as a mentor to postgraduate students, and speaking at schools. She is very proud of two of her many "adopted" daughters, one who will graduate as a doctor in June 2000 and the other, a working clown and pole climber. Lucki always liked to act and her "daughter" the clown introduced her to the producers of the Bay Area's production of the *Vagina Monologues*. She tried out for the role of The Flood, won the part and this year it was hers without an audition. Lucki says, and from everything she does, "I don't look like a little old lady and I don't act like a little old lady."

Karen Offut
WAC
(Women's Army Corps)
Stenographer, MACV

Only nineteen years of age when she joined the army, Karen Offut had to get permission from her reluctant and unhappy parents to enter the military. After basic training and an assign-

ment at the Pentagon, she was off to South Vietnam. Soon after her arrival, she found herself in Long Binh, the huge American supply and headquarters complex near Saigon, home away from home for more than fifty thousand soldiers. Long Binh, twenty miles northeast of Saigon, was frequently under enemy fire. After a short time at Long Binh, she went to Saigon and worked near Tan Son Nhut, also under frequent mortar attack, at MACV (Military Assistance Command Saigon), assigned to the generals, taking dictation as a stenographer.

I had joined the army, and at the time of the war, I was working at the Pentagon. I was nineteen years old, there was a lot of

254

controversy going on, people were protesting and it was really confusing because I believed in what we were doing. That we were fighting communism and trying to help these people that were oppressed and if communism spread from one country to another then eventually it would hit America. I believed in the whole cause and the more I thought about it, I thought that not only men should be sacrificing their lives or putting themselves in harm's way—that I could do that too, and maybe spare someone else going over. You had to volunteer to go. Basically that's why I went. Because I worked at the Pentagon I knew a lot of higher-ups, so I had to beg for quite a while because I was only nineteen years old. I think it was protective. They wanted to protect me as a woman, as a young girl. I just kept on asking, and being persistent, and I'm very tenacious. I think they just wanted to get rid of me, finally, because I kept begging to go over. I'm one of only about five hundred WACs who went over, period. I was in a small minority of the women who went.

My parents weren't real happy. I really didn't even know where Vietnam was, and I'm not sure my family did either, but they saw all the news. There were a lot of things that were televised and they were not very happy but they respected me for wanting to go.

I flew out of California, and my family was there and my brother and my parents, and there was a lot of crying. I was trying to be real brave and cool about it all, but inside I was scared. I got on the plane finally and didn't know if I'd ever see my family again. It was something I was willing to do, but when the reality hits you that you really might not ever get to hold them again, it was very difficult. We stopped over once, I believe in Hawaii, to let part of the group off who were going to Guam.

I was a little, tiny thing, very sheltered in my life. I just sat there on the plane, tears running down my face, and I remember an air force male was sitting next to me and he was real nice to me and talked to me the whole way until he got off in Hawaii to go to Guam, but I felt very isolated already because I was the only woman there on the plane.

I was born in the South, in Arkansas, and then I lived primarily in California. My older brother had died when he was young, and my other brother was also sickly. He had asthma, so I knew he wouldn't go in the service. Probably he wouldn't qualify, so that was one of the reasons that I joined initially. My parents, have been together, gosh, I think, fifty-four years, now. So it's a real close family, and I wasn't exposed to the ways of the world. It was something to get on a plane and go leave your whole family and everybody that you've always known and loved. Then to be the only woman and you don't really have a girlfriend sitting next to you to say, "What do you think is going to happen?" is difficult. I had no idea what it was going to be like. We weren't really told anything about it and what it was going to be like. The only training we had was in basic training, where we had a bivouac and where we learned to use a compass and low crawl and things like that, but I didn't know anything about Vietnam.

I think my friends thought I was crazy but I just thought it was real and the honorable thing to do. Absolutely, absolutely, I believed in it and I believed in what I was doing and I was representing my family. I just didn't see any differentiation between the men and the women as opposed to why should someone be putting their life on the line and not me just because I happened to be a female? I didn't know anything about women's lib. I just knew that it didn't seem right for me not to go. I'm a Scorpio— pretty determined people.

We landed in Bien Hoa July the 19th, 1969, and that was an experience. A lot of my memories are gone from Vietnam because it's kind of a defense mechanism I think, but I do remember landing in Bien Hoa. It must have been in the afternoon. It was hot. I think it was always hot in Vietnam. I sent all my wool clothes home later because I found out I wouldn't need them. As we got off the plane, there were all these men standing there and they started cheering, and I thought, "They're welcoming us here," that they were happy that we were joining them. Well, they were happy because we were coming in and they were leaving, and that kind of hit me because they were so happy to be leaving. They were just ecstatic. You could see it. The other thing that I remember was that these guys were just a little bit older than I was, maybe nineteen, twenty, twenty-one, and they looked really old. Their faces... there was something about them that I didn't know what it was, but I just knew that they looked very old. You lose your youth over there.

When you're facing death every day and you're in a war zone, everything is down. You just change. You go from a child more or less to an adult, almost instantly. You accept the fact that you may get killed, and in most cases over there a lot of those guys, they probably weren't going to come home. That was all the years they were going to have, and you saw so many horrendous things that you had to step out of your youth and your childhood to be able to accept it and to endure it. I wrote a poem called "So Unyouth" and that's what I think happened over there.

As soon as I landed in Bien Hoa I was supposed to go to Saigon to work for MACV headquarters, and they put me on a bus. I thought I was going to Saigon because I didn't know one town from another. I get on this bus and they're taking me to a town called Long Binh. I remember this older man was sitting next to me and I said, "Well, what is all that chicken wire on the windows?" He kind of mumbled something, and I said, "Excuse me?" and he said, "To deflect the grenades." I remember looking behind me and saying, "Is the plane still there, can I get back on it?" It hit me that it was not going to be such a good time over there. I was naive.

I remember the few years prior to that and leading up to that. I was a song leader in high school and ASB vice president. I was in all the clubs, every club that was available, practically. I was a real outgoing person. I lettered in track, rode my horse, and I was just happy-go-lucky but very scholastically inclined. I went to college at seventeen, to a nursing school, and quit the second semester and joined the service. I have gone back since then and gotten my RN and become a nurse, but I just was always full of life. I looked forward to whatever I could do the next day, all the challenges and things.

Vietnam changed everything about me. That one year changed me more than anything in my whole life. Other than having children—I have three children—Vietnam made me realize how important each day is. It made me fearful of everything around me and distrustful of people, because over there you didn't know who was going to do what to you. It just changed my whole outlook of life. Vietnam was . . . I don't know how to describe it, except to say it was the most real year of my life. Everything was brought down to life or death. Nobody was above another person. You didn't worry about what you wore, you didn't worry about how much money you had or what kind of family you came from. It was just camaraderie, living together, working together, trying to keep each other going.

I said it was the most real year of my life. Kind of like the best of times, the worst of times, as far as the brotherhood, sisterhood, the camaraderie. Caring about one another, depending on one another for survival, emotionally and physically. It made me, and a lot of veterans that I have spoken with, distrustful. I mean, I was nineteen years old, and I was too young to even be in Saigon. They wanted you to be twenty, but I kept pushing for it and saying I was supposed to be over there working for the generals at MACV headquarters. Not only was I one of the youngest at that time, I was also the youngest enlisted person and the lowest-ranking one there. We had a lot of older women who were over there, but I kept very much to myself. We all worked different jobs. We all went our separate ways. I worked six-and-a-half days a week, twelve to fifteen hours a day. Long, long hours, and then you got called in if there was going to be an air strike or whatever was going on and they needed you to do the correspondence.

I worked for logistics first, and then I worked for several generals. We prepared air strikes and if they were going to strike at night or whatever, I would have to go in and I would take dictation. Then it would be handed around to everyone and they would do their air strikes. You took all the messages. If the secretary of defense or secretary of state came over, we would also have to make sure that they were welcome and entertain them. I was always spilling tea on them. It didn't matter which dignitary came out, I'd always ruin them. Then they also would have me fly. I would go off in a chopper and if they had a special meeting with the higher-ranking Vietnamese generals, they would take me along and I would take the Dictaphone, take it back and transcribe it. It was secretarial work but towards the end I was feeling when I was just typing up something, I was thinking, "Gosh, I'm typing, this is going to help. Tonight they're going to strike a village or they're going to do this," and it just overwhelmed me. What I was doing started hitting me. Of course, everything was changing in the United

States, too. People were still saying we shouldn't be in the war. You're trying to be real upbeat, but everybody was protesting and so it was very difficult.

I think being nineteen years old, I was scared of everybody. I mean, I was afraid of anybody, including the mama-sans who were in our place. A lot of things were booby-trapped, so we didn't know who to trust. It wasn't like we were in the field. People were killed all the time, or hit. We had gunfire all the time. We were hit in Long Binh and Saigon by rockets and mortars and things. We had a Claymore mine put in front of our place. Any time you went anywhere, you didn't know if a little child was going to come up and...they used to load the children up so when the GIs would pick them up...that was it. You came back home with a feeling of distrust for everybody. A lot of us I'll say, have post–traumatic stress disorder. Your sleep changes. You're up and down all night. You're hyper-vigilant. You don't make friends really easily. You stay isolated a lot. Not everybody ended up that way, but I did.

I don't know what I remember because I've tried for a very long time to put the pieces together. It's kind of like buying a one-thousand-piece puzzle and you get it home and you find out that there's eight hundred pieces missing and you don't even know what the picture was supposed to be. That's the way I feel. But what I do remember that strikes me as kind of horrendous for a young woman to go through, or a young anybody to go through, was my first night in a new country. I didn't have a uniform yet, I didn't have any fatigues yet, but I believe they gave me a helmet and a canteen or something. I don't remember. They gave me a couple of articles, and they said, "Now put these under your bed," so I thought, "Well, they want the stuff there for inspections, like in the states." We had, I think, about five people in our room. The monsoons were coming through, the rain was coming through, we had little pans around to catch the water. Well, pretty soon it was like, boom, boom, all through the night. The bed was shaking and I was petrified. I asked the girl over from me, I said, "What is it?" She goes, "We're being hit," and that's what they wanted the stuff there for. They wanted you to be able to get out if you needed to get to the bunker or whatever. But I was paralyzed. I thought I have just gotten in country today and I'm not going to make it through the night. I'm going to die. That was one time. You got used to it. It's hard to say you got used to things, but you got used to being hit. I taped things home to my parents and my brother and in one of those tapes you could hear it. This was when I was in Saigon. You could hear it just being hit, bam, bam. I tried to tell them all the time, don't worry about me. I said, don't worry if you hear that because they're at least a half a block or a half a mile or whatever away from me. To me that was pretty far.

I lived near Tan Son Nhut Air Base outside Saigon, and that was right off MACV headquarters there. We women lived in an old motel that also had men in it, I believe on the bottom two floors, and we took the rest of it. It had a flat roof on the top, and we would go up there and just lie down in the sun if we had a lunch half-hour or something. But we were right next to 3rd Field Hospital, so all the choppers were coming in all the time. I mean, that was a constant. The sound of a helicopter will just get my blood going more than anything. Every Vietnam veteran I know, they hear it before anybody else ever hears a chopper because that's what you had, one coming over every minute or so. Anyway, I think most of my letters and my tapes to my parents were trying to alleviate their fears that I was okay, and that it didn't really work to my advantage in the long run to be afraid. I don't think that they understood me when I got back home, or the reason I had changed, because I wasn't honest about the danger I was in.

In Saigon where we lived in this hotel, we didn't even have a bunker to go into. When you were in Long Binh the women were in a kind of a fort I called it, and they had sergeants that were in charge of them and lieutenants and things. In Saigon, the reason they wanted women to be older there was because we were on our own. As a young person there we were really on our own. We worked in different places in and around Saigon and we went to our respective jobs during the day, but we didn't have anybody in charge of us. We just went to work and lived there on our own. We had Vietnamese machine gunners guarding the building. These men were ARVN, out every so many feet in the street and we had all the barbed wire and stuff, but basically to alert us we had this one little Vietnamese man that must have been seventy years old. He had one leg, he ran our generator, and was kind of *the* generator. In fact, I learned that after I left Saigon he was killed. We had wire screens that went in a slope over the front of our place, so if they lobbed a grenade in, it would roll down. I guess one grenade made it through the wire and they told me that he was killed.

We really had no evacuation plan. We had little doors and a screen that we hooked over the window because we were so hot over there. We had nothing else. We had no guns. I didn't have a gun. A girl gave me a billy club that her boyfriend had, and I bought a sword and that was it. You were afraid but you were also afraid of your own GIs because if you see what they called a round-eye there, one of us, an American, you would have people staring at you all the time and taking your picture all the time. It just *was* really scary. It was a scary type of situation. You didn't really feel safe no matter where you went. You just felt you were out of it.

In downtown Saigon there weren't any traffic lanes. Wherever they could ride, they would ride. I hadn't seen anything like that. It was strange because there were just thousands and thousands of people and then there would be big mansions and right next to it would be these little three-sided houses or make-shift homes made out of flattened beer cans and children playing in the mud and people lying in the street and begging. It was really very hard on me, especially to see all the children who lived over there.

I found an orphanage, I'm not sure even how I found it now, and I went to it. It was in downtown Saigon run by some sisters, the nuns, and I volunteered there. I worked with the babies and the little kids and played with them and left my heart there with them. They were children who'd lost their parents in the war. A lot of them had shrapnel wounds, no legs, lots of problems, and then some of the others were just given up because they were interracial children that weren't wanted by their parents.

I went there and they had these little tables with mats on them. That's what the bigger children slept on. They had a lot of babies there too, but there was this little girl that was maybe six or seven years old. She was lying there and the tops they had were just T-shirts, little shirts and nothing else on them. It was very hot, and she had this mass of blood coming out of her. It was like a big organ, and I just freaked. I didn't know what to do for her, so I got one of the GIs to drive her over to Tan Son Nhut, to one of our hospitals, but they couldn't treat her because she was an orphan. We didn't have permission to treat her or anything, so we drove her around somewhere else and we finally found this Vietnamese clinic in town and the doctor just took this piece of gauze and just shoved this mass back into her body. I don't even know what it was, if it was hemorrhoids or what. I wasn't a nurse at the time and so I really don't know, but I remember I had this charm on that my mother had given me as a teenager and I took it off and gave it to the little girl and hugged her and kissed her and I just cried. I mean, I felt absolutely helpless for those kids.

One time I was at home in Saigon at the Medford BEQ off Vo Tanh Street and I smelled smoke. I thought our building was on fire. I remember I had shorts on and was barefoot and I started telling all the women that were on my floor to get out because we were on fire. I looked out the window and could see smoke coming. Next to our hotel there was an alleyway. Alongside both sides of the alley were those little open houses with the beer can walls, and they had over the top of each of them a bamboo-type awning that kind of meshed the two sides together where the people lived. That awning went on for a long way over all the houses, and it had caught on fire. Everybody was running back in their little houses to get their chickens and the pig and whatever else they had. They were going to die for it. I just ran down there because they were going to die, and I started pulling people out. I don't feel like I was a hero or a heroine or anything. I don't remember thinking about it. When they tried to run back in for their possessions and stuff, I just kept pulling them out. That awning thing that was over the top kept falling in because it was all on fire. There wasn't any way out of that alley because it was all just houses. Eventually some type of fire department arrived, and I just went back to my room and kind of forgot about it. By then I think I was pretty much numb to new experiences and danger and whatever, and I don't remember thinking too much about it. I think my feet got burned, but I didn't go in for medicine or for anything. Then later on they called me into MACV and said that the hamlet chief of these people had signed all these pages and put his stamp on it and stuff, and said that I was the only American woman that went in after these people. Then I sent for clothes from the United States. I had my mother and a bunch of people send clothes and things for the kids. They put me in for the Soldiers' Medal but I didn't get it because they said that they didn't usually give it to a woman for heroic action. So they gave me a certificate. They call it a Certificate of Achievement for Heroic Action. The date is January 24, 1970. I wasn't upset by that, then. I think later on I was upset because someone told me that the Soldiers' Medal is not normally given to a woman. I wasn't really upset at not getting it because I did what anybody should have done, anyway.

As I look back on it, I think it was just one more way that women feel isolated. If I ever tell anybody I was in Vietnam they think I was automatically a nurse. And I say, "No, I'm a nurse now, but I wasn't then." "Well," they say, "there weren't any women over there who weren't nurses." People don't know. We had civilians, we had USO people, Red Cross, marines, we had everybody, and yet nobody knows about us. They didn't keep a list of the women to begin with. So we've had no way to keep in touch with each other, and it hasn't been until the last two and half years since I got on the computer, when I got on the Internet that I was able to find anybody who served with me over there.

They've come a long way, baby, but, we still have a long ways to go. These women gave, I mean, they gave everything, and they were willing to give their lives to go over there. They volunteered to go over, and many of them have had a lot of suffering because they went over there. They have PTSD and there are problems with their children, and so I think it's high time that people recognize that women have been in so many wars. Look where they've been. Women have been right there.

I just remember that people got really scared towards the end of the DEROS, the time that they were going to go home, because I was told, it was like a theory that people got careless towards the end and a lot of times things happened. I've heard of guys getting shot their last day in country and people getting in wrecks. As the time went on, you felt even less safe as your time to go home came about. It was like you've been lucky so far, and you're not going to get out of here. I had a parakeet over there that was my friend, and I flew the parakeet home before me, and so that it could be quarantined and all that, and then I got home I still had the bird. So it was like I brought a little piece of Vietnam back with me. He spoke Vietnamese. It was a neat bird. It's real strange because I look back at it now and it's like we left and we didn't get the addresses and names of people that we lived with for a year, and it was kind of like you wanted to leave and yet you didn't want to leave. I cried the whole way back going to the states. I think I felt guilty that I was leaving people behind. I felt guilty that I was alive. I felt like that's where I was supposed to be, like that's where I belonged, and when I got back, I didn't ever feel like I fit in again. I didn't understand.

I think at first it was real flattering to have people stare at you and take your pictures and things like that. After a while, I remember trying to get a glass of water or something and a sandwich, I believe at MACV headquarters. They had a little cafeteria, and I couldn't get the glass up, and I would try to hold it with both hands because there were so many people staring at you, that you felt like you were on the spot all the time. Since I've been back, the only people that I feel the closest to are Vietnam veterans. I don't get close to people. I just knew that I felt like I had been dropped off another planet.

I didn't know for maybe ten years what was wrong with me

when I got back. I just felt like something was wrong with me. It wasn't until actually 1986 when I talked to other Vietnam veterans who were men, not women yet—that was still a long time to come—that I found out I wasn't crazy. What I was going through and what I had been through since I had been back was real common. I have nightmares. I'd be up all night long, or up and down, awake, asleep, awake, asleep. I was no longer the social person that I was before I went over, the cheerleader type, and all that. I was very withdrawn. I got married, I had children and all three of the children were born with cancer, epilepsy and different things wrong with them. I had a husband who was telling me it was my fault because I had been exposed to Agent Orange. He said I was the one that volunteered to go to Vietnam, so you've caused your child to have cancer. There was a lot of guilt. I wanted to go back, and I wanted to be a nurse. I felt I should have been a nurse over there. I didn't feel for many years, since I didn't know anybody who had been enlisted over there, that I really was validated by going over there. People didn't understand that I did something, I played a part, but I wasn't a nurse so it didn't count. God knows I don't even know how the nurses did what they did, but there were other people, other women were there, and we all were affected in some way or another.

I'll just say that I still feel that I had honorable intentions by going over. I won't say that I feel the same as I did prior to going. I didn't change immediately, but through the years of contacting people and seeing and knowing more about what was going on, and how many people we lost and how many suicides there have been since the soldiers have been back.... I believe in freedom and democracy and helping that underdog, but gosh, there ought to be a better way of doing it. It's just like this thing that's going on right now over in Bosnia. I don't even want to look at that. It's like history is repeating itself, and we're still killing each other, for what?

You survive. I think that's in everybody. I'm not sure I could go through it again. I think it was just wanting to get home to my family and thinking that I was doing some good over there.

Let people know that women are out there risking their lives and giving all that they can. I didn't shoulder a gun, and I didn't kill anybody with my own two hands, but I was more than willing to give my life. I feel sad. I feel sad for me and I feel sad for the other people that I've met since I've been back, because they've lost something that they'll never get back—the innocence, the trust, how to enjoy life, how to look forward to things in the future—and that is real difficult.

Though born in Pine Bluff, Arkansas, Karen Offut led a peripatetic life growing up, as her parents moved from Arkansas to Arizona to California to Oregon and back to California, seeking the best climate for her asthmatic brother. Her father once owned a chicken farm, worked for a gas company, and was a sales representative. Her mother was a home-

maker. After high school, Karen was an exchange student. After graduation she started nursing school in California. She quit in her second semester and joined the army. She arrived in Vietnam with the rank of Specialist 4 and she left with the rank of Specialist 5. Karen married while in the army but left the military to raise a family. She has three children, twin sons, Justin and Kevin, and a daughter, Kristin. All her children have had medical disabilities since birth: cancer, epilepsy, and ADHD (Attention Deficit Hyperactive Disorder). Her granddaughter also has ADHD. She believes all these problems are due to her exposure to Agent Orange while serving in Vietnam. In 1984 she completed college and became an RN. Divorced, she lives north of Tampa, Florida, surrounded by open fields, cows, horses, and her bird feeders. Karen Offutt loves to read, to spend time on the Internet, play her guitar (growing up she played eight instruments), and once enjoyed fresh water fishing, even to the extent of making her own flies when she lived in Oregon.

Acknowledgments

First, the book would not have been possible without the co-operation and blessing of all the women who are on these pages and the countless others who served in Vietnam whose spirits reside here. Peter Kaufman, publisher of TV Books, and I were having lunch discussing projects when I handed him a rough draft of several interviews that eventually became part of the book. It was not exactly pages flying over the transom, but in this day of rapid communications, it was pretty close. Within days Peter Kaufman agreed to the project and we were discussing the book that has since become *Women in Vietnam*. Special thanks to Charlie Stuart and Danielle Moscowitz of Charlie Stuart Productions in Boston who developed and produced the documentary *Women at War* for ABC News Productions and TLC, The Learning Channel. Eileen Douglas read the manuscript and my thanks go to her for her usual sharp and critical eye. At TV Books, my gratitude to Albert DePetrillo, for his calm and thoughtful editing, and to Rachel Reiss for her fine interior design of the finished book.

About the Author

RON STEINMAN, an award-winning television journalist and television documentary producer, was born in Brooklyn, majored in European history at Lafayette College, and did postgraduate work at New York University. He worked at a variety of jobs before beginning his career at NBC News, where he spent thirty-five years. He produced segments and wrote for the *Huntley-Brinkley Report* and was news editor/field producer for the news magazine *Chet Huntley Reports.* For three years he produced documentaries and worked on news specials before being named NBC bureau chief in Saigon during the Vietnam War in 1966. He also served as bureau chief in Hong Kong and London before returning to New York to oversee and produce the network's live news specials. In 1975 he joined the *Today Show,* where he spent eleven years. His duties included overseeing production of all the show's live week-long broadcasts from China, Moscow, Seoul, overseas presidential trips, and all domestic politics, primaries, and national conventions. His awards include a Peabody, a National Press Club Award, two American Women in Radio and Television Awards, five Emmy nominations, and a National Headliner Award.

He has been a freelance producer at ABC News Productions, where he wrote and produced one-hour documentaries for A&E Biography, The Discovery Channel, The History Channel, and Lifetime. He produced three hours of "The Soldier's Story," The Learning Channel's six-part series on the Vietnam War, for which he wrote a companion volume, *The Soldiers' Story.* He is currently an independent documentary filmmaker with his own company, Douglas/Steinman Productions. He is married and the father of two sons, one daughter, and one stepdaughter.